A  HAKESPEARE

The Tragedy of
Romeo
and Juliet

A Facing-pages Translation into Contemporary English

Edited by
Jonnie Patricia Mobley, Ph.D.
Drama Department
Cuesta College
San Luis Obispo, California

Revised Edition

Lorenz Educational Publishers
P.O. Box 146340, Chicago, IL 60614–6340

1597 : 1st publication

Cover border taken from the First Folio (1623)

Cover design by Tamada Brown Design, Chicago

Interior design and typesetting by David Corona Design, Dubuque

Published by Lorenz Educational Publishers. © 1999 by Lorenz Educational Publishers, P.O. Box 146340, Chicago, IL 60614–6340. All rights reserved. No part of this book may be reproduced, stored in a retrieval system, or transmitted in any form or by any means without the prior permission of Lorenz Educational Publishers.

ISBN: 1-885564-11-2

Library of Congress Card Catalog Card Number: 99–71602
Manufactured in the United States of America.
9 0 8 7 6 5 4 3 2

The Tragedy of
Romeo
and Juliet

Contents

Introduction

This volume of William Shakespeare's *The Tragedy of Romeo and Juliet* consists of two versions of the play. The first is the original, based on the *Globe* edition of 1860, which was in turn based on the Folio of 1623. And this, further, was a reprint of a still earlier edition. The second version is a translation of the original into contemporary English. In both versions spelling and punctuation have been updated, and the names of the characters have been spelled out in full for easier reading. Insights from modern scholars have been included in both versions.

The translation of *Romeo and Juliet* is not meant to take the place of the original. Instead, it is an alternative to the notes usually included in modern editions. In many editions these notes interfere with the reading of the play. Whether alongside or below the original text, the notes break the rhythm of reading and frequently force the reader to turn back to an earlier page or jump ahead to a later one. Having a translation that runs parallel to the original, line for line, allows the reader to move easily from Elizabethan to contemporary English and back again. It's simply a better way to introduce Shakespeare.

Also, this translation is suitable for performance, where notes are not available to the audience. Admittedly, a well-directed and well-acted production can do much to clarify Shakespeare's language. And yet, there will be numerous references and lines whose meanings are not accessible to many on a first hearing. What, for instance, does Juliet mean when she says, "I'll stay the circumstance"?

Shakespeare's Language

Shakespeare's language does present problems for modern readers. After all, four centuries separate us from him. During this time words have acquired new meanings or have dropped from the language altogether, and sentence structures have become less fluid. But these are solvable problems.

First of all, most of the words that Shakespeare used are still current. For those words whose meanings have changed and for those words no longer in the language, modern equivalents are found in this translation. For a small number of words—chiefly names of places, biblical and mythological characters—a glossary can be found on page 247.

The meaning of words is one problem. The position of words is another. Today, the order of words in declarative sentences is almost fixed. The subject comes first, then the verb, and finally, if there is one, the object. In Shakespeare's time, the order of words, particularly in poetic drama, was more fluid. Shakespeare has Juliet say,

But all this I did know before.

Whereas we would usually arrange the words in this order,

> But I knew all this before.

Earlier in the play, Paris says,

> Of honorable reckoning are you both.

We would probably say,

> You are both of honorable reckoning.

This does not mean that Shakespeare never uses words in what we consider normal order. As often as not, he does. Here, for instance, are Romeo and a servant in conversation,

> SERVANT   But, I pray, can you read anything you see?
> ROMEO   Ay, if I know the letters and the language.

When Shakespeare does invert the order of words, he does so for a reason or for a variety of reasons—to create a rhythm, to emphasize a word, to achieve a rhyme. Whether a play is in verse, as most of this play is, or in prose, it is still written in sentences. And that means that, despite the order, all the words needed to make complete sentences are there. If you are puzzled by a sentence, first look for the subject and then try rearranging the words in the order that you would normally use. It takes a little practice, but you will be surprised how quickly you acquire the skill.

Shakespeare sometimes separates sentence parts—subject and verb, for example—that would normally be run together. Here are some lines spoken by Benvolio, describing the encounter between Romeo and Tybalt,

> All this uttered
> With gentle breath, calm look, knees humbly bowed,
> Could not take truce with the unruly spleen
> Of Tybalt, deaf to peace,

Between the subject *this* and the verb *could not take* comes a compound prepositional phrase that interrupts the normal sequence. Again, look for the subject and then the verb and put the two together. You'll find, however, that your rearranged sentence, while clear, is not as rhythmical as Shakespeare's.

Stage Directions

In drama written for the modern stage, the playwright usually provides detailed directions for the actors—how to move and speak, what emotions to convey to an audience. In the plays of Shakespeare, stage directions are sparse. One reason for this could be that Shakespeare was a member and an owner of the company for which he wrote these plays. He was on hand to tell the other actors how to say a line or what gesture to use. Even so, the dialogue itself offers clues to actions or gestures. For example, Capulet, in Act One, breaks off his scolding of Tybalt to compliment the dancers at his party. He says,

> You're a cocky lad, aren't you?
> This behavior will harm you. I know that.
> If you disobey me then it's time—
> Oh, good dancing there, friends—you show-off

The actor playing Capulet obviously must turn from Tybalt, look to the dancers as they go by and then turn back again to continue scolding Tybalt, although the printed text contains no such stage directions.

Reading the printed play, you must be alert to whom a line of dialogue is addressed. For example, Romeo and Benvolio are strolling through the streets of Verona. When Benvolio asks Romeo if he is mad, Romeo answers,

> Not mad, but less free than a madman
> Shut up in prison, kept without my food,
> Whipped and tormented and—

Then turning to a passing servant he says,

> Good evening, fellow.

But there is no stage direction to mark this change. You have to try to picture the characters in your mind.

Solo Speeches

There is another difference between the plays of Shakespeare and most modern ones—the solo speeches. These are the asides and the soliloquies in which a character reveals what is on his or her mind. Modern dramatists seem to feel that the solo speech is artificial and unrealistic. Oddly enough, modern novelists frequently use a variety of the solo speech, and some critics feel that this convention has given the novel extra power and depth, allowing it to probe deeply into the motives of its characters. One thing is certain—Shakespeare's plays without the solo speeches would not be as powerful as they are.

The Tragedy of

Romeo and Juliet

Characters

ESCALUS, Prince of Verona

MERCUTIO, kinsman of the Prince and friend of Romeo

PARIS, kinsman of the Prince, and suitor to Juliet

MONTAGUE, head of Veronese family feuding with Capulets

LADY MONTAGUE, his wife

ROMEO, their son

BENVOLIO, nephew of Montague and friend of Romeo

ABRAHAM ⎤ servants of
BALTHASAR ⎦ Montague

CAPULET, head of Veronese family feuding with Montagues

LADY CAPULET, his wife

JULIET, their daughter

TYBALT, nephew of Lady Capulet

NURSE, to Juliet

PETER, servant to Juliet's nurse

SAMPSON ⎤ servants of
GREGORY ⎦ Capulet

FRIAR LAWRENCE ⎤ Franciscan
FRIAR JOHN ⎦ monks

APOTHECARY (PHARMACIST), of Mantua

A CHORUS (A SPEAKER)

PETRUCHIO, Tybalt's companion

PAGE, of Paris

CITIZENS OF VERONA, REVELERS, MUSICIANS, TORCHBEARERS, PAGES, WATCHMEN, SERVANTS

PROLOGUE

Enter CHORUS

Two households, both alike in dignity,

    (In fair Verona, where we lay our scene),

From ancient grudge break to new mutiny,

    Where civil blood makes civil hands unclean.

From forth the fatal loins of these two foes   5

    A pair of star-crossed lovers take their life;

Whose misadventured piteous overthrows

    Doth with their death bury their parents' strife.

The fearful passage of their death-marked love,

    And the continuance of their parents' rage,   10

Which, but their children's end, nought could remove,

    Is now the two hours' traffic of our stage;

The which if you with patient ears attend,

What here shall miss, our toil shall strive to mend.

                                            Exeunt

PROLOGUE

Enter SPEAKER

Two families, both of the nobility,

    (In fair Verona, where our play is laid)

From an ancient grudge, erupt in new hostility,

    And the blood of one with the blood of the other is shed.

From the ill-fated loins of these two foes   5

    A pair of star-crossed lovers are born;

Whose unfortunate and pitiful woes

    Do only with death bury their parents' scorn.

The fearful course of this foredoomed love

    And of the parents' continuing rage,   10

Which nothing but their children's death could move,

    Is for two hours the subject of our stage;

And, if you listen with patience and with care,

What's unsaid here, our acting will then make clear.

                                        Exit

Act One

Scene 1 [*Verona. A public place*]

Enter SAMPSON *and* GREGORY, *servants of the House of Capulet, with swords and bucklers*

SAMPSON Gregory, upon my word, we'll not carry coals.

GREGORY No, for then we should be colliers.

SAMPSON I mean, an we be in choler, we'll draw.

GREGORY Ay, while you live, draw your neck out of collar.

SAMPSON I strike quickly, being moved.   5

GREGORY But thou art not quickly moved to strike.

SAMPSON A dog of the house of Montague moves me.

GREGORY To move is to stir; and to be valiant is to stand. Therefore,
     if thou art moved, thou runnest away.

SAMPSON A dog of that house shall move me to stand. I will take the   10
     wall of any man or maid of Montague's.

GREGORY That shows thee a weak slave, for the weakest goes to the
     wall.

SAMPSON 'Tis true, and therefore women being the weaker vessels are
     ever thrust to the wall. Therefore, I will push Montague's men from
     the wall, and thrust his maids to the wall.   15

GREGORY The quarrel is between our masters and us their men.

SAMPSON 'Tis all one. I will show myself a tyrant. When I have
     fought with the men, I will be civil with the maids—I will cut off
     their heads.

GREGORY The heads of the maids?   20

SAMPSON Ay, the heads of the maids, or their maidenheads—take it
     in what sense thou wilt.

GREGORY They must take it in the sense that feel it.

Act One

Scene 1 [*Verona. A public place*]

Enter SAMPSON *and* GREGORY, *servants of the House of Capulet, with swords and small shields*

SAMPSON Gregory, upon my word, we'll not stoop to carrying out coals.

GREGORY No, for then we should be coal miners.

SAMPSON I mean, if we're in a choler, we'll draw our swords.

GREGORY Yes, if your neck's in a collar, you'll have to withdraw.

SAMPSON I strike quickly once I'm provoked.   5

GREGORY But you are not easily provoked.

SAMPSON A dog from the house of Montague provokes me.

GREGORY To be provoked is to arouse; and to be virile is to stand tall; therefore, if you are provoked, you run off.

SAMPSON A dog of that house shall provoke me to stand tall. I will   10
push to the wall any man or maid of Montague's.

GREGORY That shows you to be a weakling, for the weakest goes to the wall.

SAMPSON That's true, and because they're weaker, women are always
thrust to the wall. Therefore, I will push Montague's men from
the wall and thrust his maids against the wall.   15

GREGORY The quarrel is between our masters and us, their men.

SAMPSON It's all the same. I will show myself to be a tyrant. After I have
fought the men, I will be gentle to the maids—I will cut off
their heads.

GREGORY The heads of the maids?   20

SAMPSON Yes, the heads of the maids, or their maidenheads—take it
in whatever sense you will.

GREGORY They will surely take it in one sense—those who feel it.

SAMPSON Me they shall feel while I am able to stand, and 'tis
    known I am a pretty piece of flesh.   25

GREGORY 'Tis well thou are not fish; if thou hadst, thou hadst
    been poor-john. Draw thy tool, here comes two of the house of
    Montagues.

Enter ABRAHAM *and another* SERVANT

SAMPSON My naked weapon is out. Quarrel, I will back thee.

GREGORY How, turn thy back and run?   30

SAMPSON Fear me not.

GREGORY No, marry, I fear thee!

SAMPSON Let us take the law of our sides; let them begin.

GREGORY I will frown as I pass by, and let them take it as they list.

SAMPSON Nay, as they dare. I will bite my thumb at them, which is   35
    a disgrace if they bear it.

ABRAHAM Do you bite your thumb at us, sir?

SAMPSON I do bite my thumb, sir.

ABRAHAM Do you bite your thumb at us, sir?

SAMPSON [*Aside to* GREGORY] Is the law on our side if I say "Ay"?   40

GREGORY [*Aside to* SAMPSON] No.

SAMPSON No, sir, I do not bite my thumb at you, sir, but I bite my
    thumb, sir.

GREGORY Do you quarrel, sir?

ABRAHAM Quarrel, sir? No, sir.   45

SAMPSON But if you do, sir, I am for you. I serve as good a man
    as you.

ABRAHAM No better.

SAMPSON Well, sir.

Enter BENVOLIO

SAMPSON They shall feel it as long as I am erect, and it's well known
    that I am a very manly person.   25

GREGORY It's a good thing you're not a fish; if you were, you would
    have been a piker. Draw your weapon; here come two of the house of
    Montague.

Enter ABRAHAM *and another* SERVANT

SAMPSON My naked weapon is out. Begin a quarrel, and I will back you.

GREGORY How? Turn your back and run?   30

SAMPSON Don't worry about me.

GREGORY No, indeed, I'm afraid of you.

SAMPSON Let us keep the law on our side; let them begin.

GREGORY I will frown as I go by, and let them take it as they wish.

SAMPSON No, as they dare. I will thumb my nose at them, which is   35
    an insult if they stand for it.

ABRAHAM Do you thumb your nose at us, sir?

SAMPSON I do thumb my nose, sir.

ABRAHAM Do you thumb your nose at us, sir?

SAMPSON [*Aside to* GREGORY] Is the law on our side if I say "Yes"?   40

GREGORY [*Aside to* SAMPSON] No.

SAMPSON No, sir, I do not thumb my nose at you, sir, but I thumb
    my nose, sir.

GREGORY Do you want to start a fight, sir?

ABRAHAM Start a fight, sir? No, sir.   45

SAMPSON Because if you do, sir, I am ready. My master is as
    good as yours.

ABRAHAM But no better.

SAMPSON Well, sir.

Enter BENVOLIO

(nephew of montague)

GREGORY [*Aside to* SAMPSON] Say "better." Here comes one of   50
my master's kinsmen.

SAMPSON Yes, better, sir.

ABRAHAM You lie.

SAMPSON Draw, if you be men. Gregory, remember thy swashing
blow.   55

They fight

BENVOLIO Part, fools. [*Beats down their swords*]
Put up your swords, you know not what you do.

Enter TYBALT

TYBALT What, are thou drawn among these heartless hinds?
Turn thee Benvolio, look upon thy death.

BENVOLIO I do but keep the peace. Put up thy sword,   60
Or manage it to part these men with me.

TYBALT What, drawn and talk of peace? I hate the word,
As I hate hell, all Montagues, and thee.
Have at thee coward!

They fight

Enter three or four CITIZENS *with clubs and partisans*

CITIZENS Clubs, bills, and partisans! Strike, beat them down.   65
Down with the Capulets! Down with the Montagues!

Enter old CAPULET *and* LADY CAPULET

CAPULET What noise is this? Give me my long sword, ho!

LADY CAPULET A crutch, a crutch! Why call you for a sword?

CAPULET My sword I say! Old Montague is come,
And flourishes his blade in spite of me.   70

Enter old MONTAGUE *and* LADY MONTAGUE

MONTAGUE Thou villain Capulet! Hold me not, let me go.

GREGORY [*Aside to* SAMPSON] Say "better." Here comes one of our   50
    master's relatives. *(Aren't they servants of Capulet?)*
SAMPSON Yes, better, sir. *refering to Benvolio???*

ABRAHAM You lie.

SAMPSON Draw your swords, if you are men. Gregory, remember your
    slashing blow.   55

They fight

BENVOLIO Stop it, you fools! [*Beats down their swords*]
    Put away your swords. You don't know what you're doing.

                      Enter TYBALT *(nephew of Lady Capulet)*

TYBALT What, are you fighting among these leaderless deer?
    Turn, Benvolio, and face your death.

BENVOLIO I only keep the peace. Put up your sword,   60
    Or use it to separate these men with me.

TYBALT What, a drawn sword and talk of peace? I hate the word,
    As I hate hell, all Montagues, and you.
    Fight, you coward!

They fight

      Enter three or four CITIZENS *with clubs and spears*

CITIZENS Clubs, axes, and spears! Strike, beat them down.   65
    Down with the Capulets! Down with the Montagues!

      Enter old CAPULET *and* LADY CAPULET

CAPULET What's all this noise? Give me my long sword, now!

LADY CAPULET A crutch, more likely! Why do you call for a sword?

CAPULET My sword I say! Old Montague is coming,
    And flourishes his blade to spite me.   70

      Enter old MONTAGUE *and* LADY MONTAGUE

MONTAGUE You villain Capulet! Don't hold me. Let me go.

LADY MONTAGUE Thou shalt not stir one foot to seek a foe.

Enter PRINCE ESCALUS, *with his retinue*

PRINCE Rebellious subjects, enemies to peace,

    Profaners of this neighbor-stained steel—

    Will they not hear?—What ho! You men, you beasts,   75

    That quench the fire of your pernicious rage,

    With purple fountains issuing from your veins,

    On pain of torture, from those bloody hands

    Throw your mistempered weapons to the ground,

    And hear the sentence of your moved Prince.   80

    Three civil brawls bred of an airy word,

    By thee old Capulet, and Montague,

    Have thrice disturbed the quiet of our streets,

    And made Verona's ancient citizens

    Cast by their grave beseeming ornaments,   85

    To wield old partisans, in hands as old,

    Cankered with peace, to part your cankered hate.

    If ever you disturb our streets again,

    Your lives shall pay the forfeit of the peace.

    For this time all the rest depart away.   90

    You Capulet, shall go along with me.

    And Montague, come you this afternoon,

    To know our further pleasure in this case,

    To old Freetown, our common judgment-place.

    Once more, on pain of death, all men depart.   95

Exeunt all but MONTAGUE, LADY MONTAGUE, *and* BENVOLIO

MONTAGUE Who set this ancient quarrel new abroach?

    Speak nephew, were you by when it began?

LADY MONTAGUE You shall not move a foot to start a fight.

Enter PRINCE ESCALUS, *with his attendants*

PRINCE Rebellious subjects, enemies of peace,

You stain your steel with your neighbors' blood—

Won't they listen?—Stop, now! You men, you beasts,   75

You who quench the fire of your destructive rage

With purple fountains spurting from your veins.

On pain of torture, throw down those misused weapons

From your bloody hands to the ground

And hear the sentence of your angered Prince.   80

Three public brawls, caused by some foolish words,

From you, old Capulet, and Montague,

Have thrice disturbed the quiet of our streets

And made Verona's leading citizens

Discard their sober and appropriate dress,   85

To wield old weaponry, in hands as old,

Rust-eaten with disuse, to share your festering hate.

If ever you disturb our streets again,

Your lives will pay the price to break the peace.

For now, all of you depart—away.   90

You, Capulet, will go along with me,

And Montague, come back this afternoon,

To learn our further pleasure in this case,

To old Freetown, our public judgment place.

Once more, on pain of death, all of you leave.   95

Exit all except MONTAGUE, LADY MONTAGUE, *and* BENVOLIO

MONTAGUE Who brought this old feud back to life again?

Speak, nephew, were you here when it began?

BENVOLIO Here were the servants of your adversary,
    And yours, close fighting ere I did approach.
    I drew to part them; in the instant came   100
    The fiery Tybalt, with his sword prepared,
    Which as he breathed defiance to my ears,
    He swung about his head and cut the winds,
    Who, nothing hurt withal, hissed him in scorn.
    While we were interchanging thrusts and blows,   105
    Came more and more, and fought on part and part.
    Till the Prince came, who parted either part.
LADY MONTAGUE O where is Romeo? Saw you him today?
    Right glad I am he was not at this fray.
BENVOLIO Madam, an hour before the worshipped sun   110
    Peered forth the golden window of the east,
    A troubled mind drave me to walk abroad,
    Where, underneath the grove of sycamore,
    That westward rooteth from this city side,
    So early walking did I see your son.   115
    Towards him I made; but he was 'ware of me,
    And stole into the covert of the wood.
    I, measuring his affections by my own,
    Which then most sought where most might not be found,
    Being one too many by my weary self,   120
    Pursued my humor, not pursuing his,
    And gladly shunned who gladly fled from me.
MONTAGUE Many a morning hath he there been seen,
    With tears augmenting the fresh morning's dew,
    Adding to clouds more clouds with his deep sighs,   125

Act One, Scene 1

Benvolio persuades Romeo to go to the feast

(Romeo's cousin)

BENVOLIO Here were some men who serve your enemy,

And your own men, fighting hard as I approached.

I drew my sword to part them; at that moment,   100

The fiery Tybalt came with his sword ready,

Which, as he swore defiance to my ears,

He swung about his head, and sliced the air.

The air, not being hurt, hissed him in scorn.

While we were exchanging thrusts and blows,   105

More and more people came to fight on this side and that

Until the Prince came and parted side from side.

LADY MONTAGUE Oh, where is Romeo? Have you seen him today?

I am glad he was not in this fray.

BENVOLIO Madam, an hour before the glorious sun   110

Shone through the golden window of the east,

A troubled mind drove me to take a walk

Where, underneath the grove of sycamore, ?

That grows far to the west of this city,

There also walking early, I could see your son.   115

I walked toward him, but he saw me coming,

And hid inside a thicket of the woods.

I, measuring his feelings by my own,

Which then most wished to be where most were not,

Being one too many by my own sad self,   120

Pursued my own desire, ignoring his,

And gladly shunned him who gladly hid from me.

MONTAGUE Many a morning has he been seen there,

His tears adding to the fresh morning's dew,

Adding gloom to more gloom with his deep sighs,   125

But all so soon as the all-cheering sun
Should in the farthest east begin to draw
The shady curtains from Aurora's bed,
Away from light steals home my heavy son,
And private in his chambers pens himself,   130
Shuts up his windows, locks fair daylight out,
And makes himself an artificial night.
Black and portentous must this humor prove,
Unless good counsel may the cause remove.

BENVOLIO My noble uncle, do you know the cause?   135
MONTAGUE I neither know it, nor can learn of him.
BENVOLIO Have you importuned him by any means?
MONTAGUE Both by myself and many other friends.
But he, his own affections' counsellor,
Is to himself—I will not say how true—   140
But to himself so secret and so close,
So far from sounding and discovery,
As is the bud bit with an envious worm,
Ere he can spread his sweet leaves to the air,
Or dedicate his beauty to the sun.   145
Could we but learn from whence his sorrows grow,
We would as willingly give cure as know.

Enter ROMEO

BENVOLIO See where he comes. So please you, step aside.
I'll know his grievance or be much denied.
MONTAGUE I would thou wert so happy by thy stay,   150
To hear true shift. Come madam, let's away.

Exeunt MONTAGUE *and* LADY MONTAGUE

But just as soon as the all-cheering sun
Would in the farthest east begin to draw
The dark curtains from the bed of dawn,
My sad son creeps home, away from the light.
He pens himself up in his room alone,   130
Shutters his windows, keeps the bright day out,
And creates for himself an artificial night.
This mood must dark and ominous prove
Unless good advice can the cause remove.

BENVOLIO My noble uncle, do you know the cause?   135

MONTAGUE I neither know it nor can learn it from him.

BENVOLIO Have you asked him about it?

MONTAGUE Yes, I have and so have many other friends,
But he keeps all his feelings to himself,
Takes no advice—I don't know if that is good—   140
But keeps to himself, so secret and withdrawn.
I'm far from knowing what it's all about.
He's like the bud eaten by a malicious worm,
Before its lovely leaves can open up to air
And dedicate its beauty to the sun.   145
If we could only learn from where his sorrows grow,
We'd be as glad to find a cure as know.

Enter ROMEO

BENVOLIO See, here he comes. If you please, step aside.
I'll learn his grief or firmly be denied.

MONTAGUE By staying here I hope you'll get to know   150
What troubles him. Come madam, let us go.

Exit MONTAGUE *and* LADY MONTAGUE

BENVOLIO Good morrow, cousin.

ROMEO Is the day so young?

BENVOLIO But new struck nine.

ROMEO Ay me, sad hours seem long.   155

    Was that my father that went hence so fast?

BENVOLIO It was. What sadness lengthens Romeo's hours?

ROMEO Not having that which, having, makes them short.

BENVOLIO In love?

ROMEO Out—   160

BENVOLIO Of love?

ROMEO Out of her favor where I am in love.

BENVOLIO Alas that love, so gentle in his view,

    Should be so tyrannous and rough in proof!

ROMEO Alas that love, whose view is muffled still,   165

    Should without eyes see pathways to his will.

    Where shall we dine? O me, what fray was here?

    Yet tell me not, for I have heard it all.

    Here's much to do with hate, but more with love.

    Why then, O brawling love, O loving hate,   170

    O any thing of nothing first created!

    O heavy lightness, serious vanity,

    Misshapen chaos of well-seeming forms,

    Feather of lead, bright smoke, cold fire, sick health,

    Still-waking sleep, that is not what it is!   175

    This love feel I, that feel no love in this.

    Dost thou not laugh?

BENVOLIO No coz, I rather weep.

ROMEO Good heart, at what?

BENVOLIO At thy good heart's oppression.   180

BENVOLIO Good morning, cousin.

ROMEO Is the day so young?

BENVOLIO Just now struck nine.

ROMEO Oh me, sad hours seem long.   155

    Was that my father who left here so fast?

BENVOLIO It was. What sadness lengthens your hours, Romeo?

ROMEO Not having that, which having, would make them short.

BENVOLIO You're in love?

ROMEO Out—   160

BENVOLIO Of love?

ROMEO Out of her favor with whom I'm in love.

BENVOLIO It's sad that love, so gentle in appearance,

    Should prove so merciless and cruel in experience.

ROMEO It's sad that love, and blind love still,   165

    Should without eyes find ways to force its will.

    Where shall we dine? Oh, my, what fight happened here?

    Oh no, don't tell me, for I've heard it all.

    Here's much to do with hate, but more with love:

    So then, Oh, brawling love! Oh, loving hate!   170

    Oh, all things were from nothing first created!

    Oh, heavy lightness, serious silliness,

    Formless mass of pretty looking forms,

    Feather of lead, clear smoke, cold fire, sick health,

    A wakeful sleep, that is not what it is!   175

    This love I have in which I have no love.

    Are you laughing?

BENVOLIO No, cousin, weeping, rather.

ROMEO Good friend, at what?

BENVOLIO At your good heart's depression.   180

ROMEO   Why, such is love's transgression.

    Griefs of mine own lie heavy in my breast,

    Which thou wilt propagate to have it pressed

    With more of thine. This love that thou hast shown

    Doth add more grief to too much of mine own.   185

    Love is a smoke made with the fume of sighs,

    Being purged, a fire sparkling in lovers' eyes,

    Being vexed, a sea nourished with lovers' tears.

    What is it else? A madness most discreet,

    A choking gall, and a preserving sweet.   190

    Farewell my coz.

BENVOLIO   Soft, I will go along.

    And if you leave me so, you do me wrong.

ROMEO   Tut I have lost myself; I am not here.

    This is not Romeo, he's some other where.   195

BENVOLIO   Tell me in sadness, who is that you love?

ROMEO   What, shall I groan and tell thee?

BENVOLIO   Groan? Why no.

    But sadly tell me who.

ROMEO   Bid a sick man in sadness make his will?   200

    A word ill urged to one that is so ill.

    In sadness cousin, I do love a woman.

BENVOLIO   I aimed so near when I supposed you loved.

ROMEO   A right good mark-man. And she's fair I love.

BENVOLIO   A right fair mark, fair coz, is soonest hit.   205

ROMEO   Well in that hit you miss. She'll not be hit

    With Cupid's arrow. She hath Dian's wit,

    And, in strong proof of chastity well armed,

    From Love's weak childish bow she lives uncharmed.

ROMEO Why such is love's wrong.

    Griefs of my own lie heavy on my heart,

    Which you only multiply, make me more depressed,

    With more of yours. This sympathy you've shown

    Adds more grief to too much of my own.   185

    Love is a smoke that rises from the fumes of sighs,

    When cleared reveals a fiery spark in lovers' eyes,

    When thwarted, a sea fed with loving tears.

    What else is it? A madness most wise,

    A gagging poison, and a nourishing sweet.   190

    Farewell, my cousin.

BENVOLIO Wait, I will go with you;

    To leave me here like this is wrong to do.

ROMEO Nonsense, I just lost myself. I am not here.

    This is not Romeo, he's some other place.   195

BENVOLIO Tell me, seriously, who is it that you love?

ROMEO What, should I groan, and then tell you?

BENVOLIO Groan? Why no;

    But, seriously, tell me who.

ROMEO Would you ask a sick man, seriously, to make his will?   200

    An ill choice of words for someone who is so ill.

    But, seriously, cousin, I love a woman.

BENVOLIO I hit that target when I heard you were in love.

ROMEO A good marksman. And she's beautiful, the one I love.

BENVOLIO An easy target, dear cousin, is easiest hit.   205

ROMEO Well, in that shot you miss. She'll not be hit

    With Cupid's arrow. She has Diana's wit

    And is well-protected by the armor of chastity.

    From the weak, childish bow of Cupid, she's safe.

She will not stay the siege of loving terms,   210

Nor bide the encounter of assailing eyes,

Nor ope her lap to saint-seducing gold.

O she is rich in beauty, only poor

That, when she dies, with beauty dies her store.

BENVOLIO Then she hath sworn that she will live chaste?   215

ROMEO She hath, and in that sparing makes huge waste;

For beauty, starved with her severity,

Cuts beauty off from all posterity.

She is too fair, too wise; wisely too fair,

To merit bliss by making me despair.   220

She hath forsworn to love, and in that vow

Do I live dead that live to tell it now.

BENVOLIO Be ruled by me, forget to think of her.

ROMEO O teach me how I should forget to think.

BENVOLIO By giving liberty to thine eyes.   225

Examine other beauties.

ROMEO 'Tis the way

To call hers, exquisite, in question more.

These happy masks that kiss fair ladies' brows,

Being black, puts us in mind they hide the fair.   230

He that is strucken blind cannot forget

The precious treasure of his eyesight lost.

Show me a mistress that is passing fair,

What doth her beauty serve, but as a note

Where I may read who passed that passing fair?   235

Farewell, thou canst not teach me to forget.

BENVOLIO I'll pay that doctrine, or else die in debt.

Exeunt

She will not listen to my loving words, 210

Nor let me look at her with loving eyes,

Nor be bought by gold that would seduce a saint.

Oh, she is rich in beauty, but poor

In that, when she dies, her beauty will die with her.

BENVOLIO Then she has sworn that she will always be a virgin? 215

ROMEO She has, and in holding back her love, is stingily wasteful;

For beauty, starved from severity,

Cuts beauty off from all posterity.

She is too beautiful, too wise, too wisely beautiful

To earn heaven by making me despair. 220

She has sworn off love, and in that vow

Do I live dead and live to tell it now.

BENVOLIO Take my advice: forget. Don't think of her.

ROMEO Oh, teach me how I can forget to think.

BENVOLIO By looking elsewhere with your eyes. 225

Look at other beauties.

ROMEO That's the way

To bring hers, exquisite, more to my mind.

Those lucky masks whose brims hug pretty ladies' brows,

Remind us that black shadows can hide beauty. 230

Anyone struck blind cannot forget

The precious treasure of his eyesight lost.

Show me a woman of exceeding beauty,

What purpose does it serve? It's a reminder

Of her who is still more beautiful than she. 235

Farewell, you cannot teach me to forget.

BENVOLIO I'll bet I can, or else die in debt.

They exit

Scene 2 [*The same place. That afternoon*]

Enter CAPULET, PARIS, *and a* SERVANT

CAPULET But Montague is bound as well as I,

In penalty alike; and 'tis not hard, I think,

For men so old as we to keep the peace.

PARIS Of honorable reckoning are you both,

And pity 'tis you lived at odds so long.   5

But now my lord, what say you to my suit?

CAPULET But saying o'er what I have said before.

My child is yet a stranger in the world,

She hath not seen the change of fourteen years.

Let two summers more wither in their pride   10

Ere we may think her ripe to be a bride.

PARIS Younger than she are happy mothers made.

CAPULET And too soon marred are those so early made.

Earth hath swallowed all my hopes but she,

She is the hopeful lady of my earth.   15

But woo her, gentle Paris, get her heart;

My will to her consent is but a part.

And she agreed, within her scope of choice

Lies my consent and fair according voice.

This night I hold an old accustomed feast,   20

Whereto I have invited many a guest,

Such as I love; and you among the store,

One more, most welcome, makes my number more.

At my poor house look to behold this night

Earth-treading stars that make dark heaven light.   25

Such comfort as do lusty young men feel

When well-apparelled April on the heel

Scene 2 [*The same place. That afternoon*] suitor to Juliet
Enter CAPULET, PARIS, *and a* SERVANT

CAPULET But Montague is bound as well as I,

    The penalty's the same; and it's not hard, I think,

    For men as old as we to keep the peace.

PARIS Of honored reputation are you both,

    It's a pity you have lived at odds so long,   5

    But now, what do you say to my proposal?

CAPULET I'll say again what I have said before:

    My child is unfamiliar with the world,

    She has not seen the change of fourteen years.

    Let two more summers wither in their pride,   10

    Before we think her ripe to be a bride.

PARIS Younger than she have become happy mothers.

CAPULET And too soon ruined are those so early made.

    Earth has swallowed all my hopes but her;

    This lady's all the hope I have on earth.   15

    But court her, gentle Paris, win her heart;

    My will is but a part of her consent.

    If she agrees, within her scope of choice

    Lies my consent and full approving voice.

    Tonight I hold my customary feast,   20

    To which I have invited many a guest,

    All those I love; and you among the rest,

    One more, most welcome, my distinguished guest.

    At my poor house expect to see this night

    Earth-walking stars that make dark heaven bright.   25

    Such pleasure as do lusty young men feel

    When well-dressed April on the heel

Of limping winter treads, even such delight
Among fresh female buds shall you this night
Inherit at my house. Hear all, all see,   30
And like her most whose merit most shall be;
Which on more view, of many—mine being one—
May stand in number, though in reckoning none.
Come, go with me.

[*To* SERVANT, *giving a paper*] Go sirrah, trudge about   35
Through fair Verona, find those persons out
Whose names are written there, and to them say,
My house and welcome on their pleasure stay.

              [*Exeunt* CAPULET and PARIS]

SERVANT Find them out whose names are written here! It
is written that the shoemaker should meddle with his yard,   40
and the tailor with his last, the fisher with his pencil, and
the painter with his nets. But I am sent to find those persons
whose names are here writ, and can never find what names
the writing person hath here writ. I must to the learned. In
good time.   45

           Enter BENVOLIO *and* ROMEO

BENVOLIO Tut man, one fire burns out another's burning,
One pain is lessened by another's anguish;
Turn giddy, and be holp by backward turning;
One desperate grief cures with another's languish.
Take thou some new infection to thy eye,   50
And the rank poison of the old will die.

ROMEO Your plantain leaf is excellent for that.

BENVOLIO For what I pray thee?

ROMEO For your broken shin.

Of lingering winter treads, just such delight
Among fresh female buds will you tonight
Enjoy within my house. Hear all, all see,   30
And love her most whose worth seems most to be.
And on viewing more—mine you shall also see—
Many may stand in number, though mine of no account be.
Come, go with me.
[*To* SERVANT, *giving a paper*] You there, go trudge about   35
Through our Verona, seek those persons out
Whose names are written here, and to them state
My house and welcome on their pleasure wait.

                             [*Exit* CAPULET *and* PARIS]

SERVANT Find them out whose names are written here! I
    know that the shoemaker should work with his yardstick,   40
    and the tailor with his leather, the fisherman with his pencil,
    and the painter with his nets; but I am sent to find out those
    persons whose names are written here when I cannot read
    what the writer wrote. I must find someone who can read.
    Well, this is good timing.   45

                Enter BENVOLIO *and* ROMEO

BENVOLIO Nonsense, man, one fire burns out another.
    One's pain is lessened by another pain;
    If you turned till dizzy, then reverse your turning;
    One desperate grief's cured with another woe.
    Find yourself a new infection for your eyes   50
    And the poison of the old infection dies.

ROMEO The plantain leaf is a good remedy for that.

BENVOLIO For what, may I ask?

ROMEO For your broken bone.

BENVOLIO Why Romeo, art thou mad?   55

ROMEO Not mad, but bound more than a madman is;

    Shut up in prison, kept without my food,

    Whipped and tormented, and—God-den good fellow.

SERVANT God gi' god-den. I pray, sir, can you read?

ROMEO Ay, mine own fortune in my misery.   60

SERVANT Perhaps you have learned it without book.

    But, I pray, can you read anything you see?

ROMEO Ay, if I know the letters and the language.

SERVANT Ye say honestly; rest you merry.

ROMEO Stay fellow, I can read. [*takes the list and reads*]   65

    "Signior Martino, and his wife and daughters; County Anselme,

    and his beauteous sisters; the lady widow of Vitruvio; Signior

    Placentio, and his lovely nieces; Mercutio, and his brother Valentine;

    mine uncle Capulet, his wife, and daughters; my fair niece Rosaline,

    and Livia; Signior Valentino, and his cousin Tybalt; Lucio, and the

    lively Helena."   70

    A fair assembly. Whither should they come?

SERVANT Up.

ROMEO Whither?

SERVANT To supper; to our house.

ROMEO Whose house?   75

SERVANT My master's.

ROMEO Indeed I should have asked you that before.

SERVANT Now I'll tell you without asking. My master is the great rich

    Capulet; and if you be not of the house of Montagues, I pray come

    and crush a cup of wine. Rest you merry.   80

Exit

BENVOLIO At this same ancient feast of Capulet's

    Sups the fair Rosaline whom thou so lovest,

BENVOLIO Why, Romeo, are you mad?   55
ROMEO Not mad, but less free than a madman
    Shut up in prison; kept without my food,
    Whipped and tormented, and—Good evening, fellow.
SERVANT Good evening, sir. Tell me, can you read?
ROMEO Yes, my own fortune in my misery.   60
SERVANT Maybe you pretend to read something you've memorized.
    But tell me, can you read anything you see?
ROMEO Yes, if I know the letters and the language.
SERVANT You speak honestly. Goodbye.
ROMEO Wait, fellow, I can read. [*takes the list and reads*]   65
    "Signior Martino and his wife and daughters; Count Anselme and
    his beauteous sisters; the lady widow of Vitruvio; Signior Placentio
    and his lovely nieces; Mercutio and his brother Valentine; my Uncle
    Capulet, his wife, and daughters; my fair niece Rosaline, and Livia;
    Signior Valentino, and his cousin Tybalt; Lucio, and the lively
    Helena."   70
    A fine assembly of people. Where are they to come?
SERVANT Up.
ROMEO Where?
SERVANT To supper. To our house.
ROMEO Whose house?   75
SERVANT My master's.
ROMEO Indeed, I should have asked you that before.
SERVANT Now I'll tell you without asking. My master is the great rich
    Capulet, and if you are not from the house of Montague, please come,
    too, and drink a glass of wine. Fare you well.   80
                                     Exit
BENVOLIO At Capulet's old customary feast,
    The lovely Rosaline, whom you love, will dine,

With all the admired beauties of Verona.

Go thither, and with unattainted eye,

Compare her face with some that I shall show,   85

And I will make thee think thy swan a crow.

ROMEO When the devout religion of mine eye

Maintains such falsehood, then turn tears to fire,

And these who, often drowned, can never die,

Transparent heretics, be burnt for liars.   90

One fairer than my love? The all-seeing sun

Ne'er saw her match since first the world begun.

BENVOLIO Tut, you saw her fair, none else being by,

Herself poised with herself in either eye.

But in that crystal scales let there be weighed   95

Your lady's love against some other maid

That I will show you shining at this feast,

And she shall scant show well that now seems best.

ROMEO I'll go along, no such sight to be shown,

But to rejoice in splendor of mine own.   100

Exeunt

Scene 3 [*A room in Capulet's house*]

Enter LADY CAPULET *and* NURSE

LADY CAPULET Nurse, where's my daughter? Call her forth to me.

NURSE Now, by my maidenhead at twelve year old,

I bade her come. What lamb! What ladybird!

God forbid! Where's this girl? What Juliet!

Enter JULIET

JULIET How now? Who calls?   5

NURSE Your mother.

With all the admired beauties of Verona.

Go, and with a true, unbiased eye,

Compare her face with others there on show,   85

And it will make you think your swan's a crow.

ROMEO When the devout belief of my own eye

Accepts such falsehood, then turn my tears to fire,

Let my eyes—often drowned but not made to die—

Like transparent heretics, be burnt as liars.   90

One fairer than my love? The all-seeing sun

Never saw her match since first the world begun.

BENVOLIO Nonsense, you think she's a beauty, because no one else is by;

She's balanced like twins in either eye,

But in your eyes, those crystal scales, let there be weighed   95

Your lady's love against some other maid

That I will show you shining at this feast,

And she shall show poorly who now seems best.

ROMEO I'll come along, not to see some better choice,

But, in the splendor of my own, rejoice.   100

Exit

Scene 3 [*A room in Capulet's house*]

Enter LADY CAPULET *and* NURSE

LADY CAPULET Nurse, where's my daughter? Tell her to come to me.

NURSE Now by my virginity when I was twelve,

I have told her to come. O lamb! O ladybird!

God forbid! Where is that girl? O Juliet!

Enter JULIET

JULIET What now? Who's calling?   5

NURSE Your mother.

JULIET Madam, I am here. What is your will?

LADY CAPULET This is the matter—Nurse, give leave awhile,
We must talk in secret. Nurse, come back again,
I have remembered me, thou's hear our counsel.   10
Thou knowest my daughter's of a pretty age.

NURSE Faith, I can tell her age unto an hour.

LADY CAPULET She's not fourteen.

NURSE I'll lay fourteen of my teeth,
And yet to my teen be it spoken, I have but four,   15
She's not fourteen. How long is it now
To Lammas-tide?

LADY CAPULET A fortnight and odd days.

NURSE Even or odd, of all days in the year,
Come Lammas Eve at night shall she be fourteen.   20
Susan and she—God rest all Christian souls—
Were of an age. Well, Susan is with God,
She was too good for me. But as I said,
On Lammas Eve at night shall she be fourteen;
That shall she. Marry, I remember it well.   25
'Tis since the earthquake now eleven years,
And she was weaned—I never shall forget it—
Of all the days of the year, upon that day.
For I had laid wormwood to my dug,
Sitting in the sun under the dovehouse wall.   30
My lord and you were then at Mantua.
Nay, I do bear a brain. But, as I said,
When it did taste the wormwood on the nipple
Of my dug, and felt it bitter, pretty fool,
To see it tetchy and fall out with the dug.   35

JULIET Madam, I am here. What do you wish?

LADY CAPULET There is a matter—Nurse, leave us awhile,

We must talk in secret. Nurse, come back again,

I've changed my mind; you'll hear our secrets.　　　　　10

You know my daughter is at a marriageable age.

NURSE Faith, I can tell her age right to the hour.

LADY CAPULET She's not fourteen.

NURSE I'll bet fourteen of my teeth,

And yet to my sorrow be it said, I have only four,　　　　15

She's not fourteen. How long is it now

To Lammastide?

LADY CAPULET Some two weeks and a few odd days.

NURSE Even or odd, of all days of the year,

At July's end at night, she shall be fourteen.　　　　20

*Susan and she—God rest all Christian souls—

Were the same age. Well, Susan is with God.

She was too good for me. But as I said,

At July's end at night, she will be fourteen;

That she shall. Truly, I remember it well.　　　　25

It's now eleven years since the earthquake,

And since she was weaned—I shall never forget it—

Of all the days of the year, just on that day.

For I had put bitters on my breast,

Sitting in the sun under the dovehouse wall.　　　　30

My lord and you were then in Mantua,

Oh, I remember it well. But, as I said,

When she did taste the bitters on the nipple

Of my breast, and it was bitter, pretty thing,

To see her angry and push away my breast.　　　　35

*Nurse's daughter - died in an EQ

31

"Shake," quoth the dovehouse. 'Twas no need, I trow,

To bid me trudge.

And since that time it is eleven years,

For then she could stand high-lone. Nay, by the rood,

She could have run and waddled all about;   40

For even the day before, she broke her brow,

And then my husband—God be with his soul,

'A was a merry man—took up the child.

"Yea," quoth he, "dost thou fall upon thy face?

Thou wilt fall backward when thou hast more wit, 45

Will thou not, Jule?" And by my holidam,

The pretty wretch left crying, and said "Ay."

To see now how a jest shall come about!

I warrant, an I should live a thousand years,

I never should forget it. "Wilt thou not?" quoth he, 50

And, pretty fool, it stinted, and said "Ay."

LADY CAPULET Enough of this. I pray thee, hold thy peace.

NURSE Yes, madam, yet I could not choose but laugh,

To think it should leave crying and say "Ay."

And yet I warrant it had upon its brow   55

A bump as big as a young cockerel's stone,

A perilous knock, and it cried bitterly.

"Yea," quoth my husband, "fallest thou upon thy face?

Thou wilt fall backward when thou comest to age:

Wilt thou not Jule?" It stinted, and said "Ay." 60

JULIET And stint thou too, I pray thee, Nurse, say I.

NURSE Peace, I have done. God mark thee to his grace;

Thou wast the prettiest babe that e'er I nursed.

And I might live to see thee married once,

Then the dovehouse shook from the earthquake. No need

To tell me to move.

And since that time, it's been eleven years,

For she could then stand alone. Why, by the holy cross,

She could then run and waddled all about,   40

For only the day before, she cut her head,

And then my husband—God be with his soul,

He was a merry man—picked up the child.

"Yes," he said, "did you fall on your face?

You'll fall backward when you grow up,   45

Will you not, Jule?" And by heavens,

The pretty thing stopped crying, and said "Yes."

To see now how a joke shall come about.

I swear, if I should live a thousand years,

I shall never forget it. "Will you not?" said he,   50

And, pretty thing, she ceased and said, "Yes."

LADY CAPULET Enough of this. Please, keep quiet.

NURSE Yes, madam, yet I could not help but laugh,

To think she should stop crying and say, "Yes."

And yet I swear she had on her head   55

A lump as big as a young rooster's rock,

A dreadful blow, and she cried bitterly.

"Yes," said my husband, "so you fell on your face?

You will fall backward when you come of age,

Will you not, Jule?" She stopped and said "Yes."   60

JULIET And you must stop, too, Nurse, I guess.

NURSE Peace, I am through. God bless you with his grace,

You were the prettiest baby that ever I nursed.

If I might live to see you married sometime,

I have my wish.   65

LADY CAPULET Marry, that "marry" is the very theme

    I came to talk of. Tell me daughter Juliet

    How stands your disposition to be married?

JULIET It is an honor that I dream not of.

NURSE An honor? Were not I thine only nurse,   70

    I would say thou hadst sucked wisdom from thy teat.

LADY CAPULET Well, think of marriage now. Younger than you,

    Here in Verona, ladies of esteem,

    Are made already mothers. By my count,

    I was your mother much upon these years   75

    That you are now a maid. Thus then in brief:

    The valiant Paris seeks you for his love.

NURSE A man, young lady; lady, such a man

    As all the world—why he's a man of wax.

LADY CAPULET Verona's summer hath not such a flower.   80

NURSE Nay he's a flower; in faith a very flower.

LADY CAPULET What say you, can you love the gentleman?

    This night you shall behold him at our feast.

    Read o'er the volume of young Paris' face,

    And find delight writ there with beauty's pen;   85

    Examine every married lineament,

    And see how one another lends content;

    And what obscured in this fair volume lies

    Find written in the margent of his eyes.

    This precious book of love, this unbound lover,   90

    To beautify him only lacks a cover.

    The fish lives in the sea, and 'tis much pride

    For fair without the fair within to hide.

I'll have my wish.   65

LADY CAPULET Indeed, marriage is the very theme

    I came to talk of. Tell me daughter, my Juliet,

    How do you feel about getting married?

JULIET It is an honor that I've never dreamed of.

NURSE An honor, if I weren't your only nurse,   70

    I would say you've sucked wisdom from your nurse's breast.

LADY CAPULET Well, think of marriage now. Younger than you,

    Here in Verona, ladies of esteem,

    Are mothers now already. If I am correct,

    I became your mother when I was your age,   75

    But you are still a maid. This, then, in brief:

    The valiant Paris wants you for his love.

NURSE A man, young lady! Lady, he is such a man

    As the entire world—why, he's a model of a man.

LADY CAPULET Verona's summer has not such a flower.   80

NURSE Nay, he's a flower; in truth, a very flower.

LADY CAPULET What do you say? Can you love the gentleman?

    Tonight you'll see him at our banquet.

    Read the book that is young Paris' face,

    You'll find joy written there with beauty's pen.   85

    Examine each and every feature,

    And see how each complements the other.

    And what's hidden in these pages lies

    Written in the margin, that is, his eyes.

    This precious unbound book of love, this lover,   90

    To be more beautiful needs only a cover.

    The fish is covered by the sea, and so

    Beauty outside hides the inner glow.

That book in many's eyes doth share the glory,

That in gold clasps locks in the golden story.   95

So shall you share all that he doth possess,

By having him, making yourself no less.

NURSE No less! Nay, bigger; women grow by men.

LADY CAPULET Speak briefly; can you like of Paris' love?

JULIET I'll look to like, if looking liking move.   100

But no more deep will I endart mine eye

Than your consent gives strength to make it fly.

Enter a SERVANT

SERVANT Madam, the guests are come, supper served up,

you called, my young lady asked for, the Nurse cursed in

the pantry, and everything in extremity. I must hence to   105

wait; I beseech you follow straight.

LADY CAPULET We follow thee.

Exit SERVANT

Juliet, the County stays.

NURSE Go girl, seek happy nights to happy days.

Exeunt

Scene 4 [*Hours later. In front of Capulet's house*]

Enter ROMEO, BENVOLIO, MERCUTIO *with five or six other*

MASKERS, *and* TORCHBEARERS

ROMEO What, shall this speech be spoke for our excuse?

Or shall we on without apology?

BENVOLIO The date is out of such prolixity.

We'll have no Cupid hoodwinked with a scarf,

Bearing a Tartar's painted bow of lath,   5

Scaring the ladies like a crow-keeper;

That book in many eyes does share the glory,

That with golden covers bind a golden story.   95

So you will share all he does possess,

By having him, it makes you not the less.

NURSE No less! Why, bigger! Women grow by men.

LADY CAPULET In short, can you like having Paris' love?

JULIET I'll look to like him, if looks can make me like him.   100

But no more deeply will my eyes dart there

Than your consent will wing them through the air.

Enter a SERVANT

SERVANT Madam, your guests have come, supper is served,

you are called for, my young lady asked for, the Nurse cursed

in the pantry, and everything is in confusion. I must go to serve;   105

I beg you to follow immediately.

LADY CAPULET We'll follow you.

Exit SERVANT

Juliet, the Count waits, please!

NURSE Go girl, seek happy nights to happy days.

They exit

Scene 4 [*Hours later. In front of Capulet's house*]

Enter ROMEO, BENVOLIO, MERCUTIO *with five or six other*

MASQUERADERS *and* TORCHBEARERS

ROMEO What, shall I give a speech to introduce us?

Or shall we just go in?

BENVOLIO Such formality is out of date.

We'll have no little boy blindfolded like Cupid

Carrying a heavy painted bow of cheap wood,   5

Frightening ladies like a scarecrow;

No nor without-book prologue, faintly spoke

After the prompter, for our entrance.

But let them measure us by what they will,

We'll measure them a measure, and be gone. 10

ROMEO   Give me a torch; I am not for this ambling.

Being but heavy, I will bear the light.

MERCUTIO   Nay gently Romeo, we must have you dance.

ROMEO   Not I, believe me; you have dancing shoes

With nimble soles; I have a soul of lead 15

So stakes me to the ground I cannot move.

MERCUTIO   You are a lover; borrow Cupid's wings,

And soar with them above a common bound.

ROMEO   I am too sore empierced with his shaft

To soar with his light feathers; and so bound, 20

I cannot bound a pitch above dull woe.

Under love's heavy burden do I sink.

MERCUTIO   And to sink in it should you burden love:

Too great oppression for a tender thing.

ROMEO   Is love a tender thing? It is too rough, 25

Too rude, too boisterous, and it pricks like thorn.

MERCUTIO   If love be rough with you, be rough with love.

Prick love for pricking, and you beat love down.

Give me a case to put my visage in. [*Puts on a mask*]

A visor for a visor. What care I 30

What curious eye doth quote deformities?

Here are the beetle brows shall blush for me.

BENVOLIO   Come knock and enter, and no sooner in,

But every man betake him to his legs.

ROMEO   A torch for me; let wantons light of heart 35

And mumbling all his lines, following

After the prompter, just so we get in.

No, let them make of us what they will,

We'll dance a dance with them and then be gone.   10

ROMEO Give me a torch; I'm not for all this dancing.

Being heavy-hearted, I will hold the light.

MERCUTIO No, gentle Romeo, we must have you dance.

ROMEO Not I, believe me; you have dancing shoes

With nimble soles; I have a soul of lead   15

That holds me to the ground so I cannot move.

MERCUTIO You are a lover; borrow Cupid's wings,

And soar with them above an ordinary bound.

ROMEO I am too sorely pierced with his shaft

To soar with his light feathers; and so bound   20

I cannot bound an inch above low spirits;

Under love's heavy burden do I sink.

MERCUTIO If you sink in it, you are love's burden;

Too great a pressing for a tender thing.

ROMEO Is love a tender thing? It is too rough,   > describing 25

Too rude, too stormy, and it pricks like thorns.   love ♀

MERCUTIO If love is rough with you, be rough with love.

Prick love for pricking, and you'll beat love down.

Give me a mask to hide my face. [*Puts on a mask*]

A mask for a mask. What do I care   30

If the curious eye notes my ugliness?

These beetlelike brows shall cover my embarrassment.

BENVOLIO Come, knock and enter, and no sooner in,

Than every man shall begin to dance.

ROMEO A torch for me; let the wild ones, light in heart,   35

Tickle the senseless rushes with their heels.

For I am proverbed with <u>grandsire phrase</u>:

I'll be a candle-holder and look on;

The game was ne'er so fair, and I am done.

MERCUTIO <u>Tut,</u> dun's the mouse, the constable's own word.   40

    If thou art Dun, we'll draw thee from the mire

    Of this, save-your-reverence, love, wherein thou sickest

    Up to the ears. Come, we burn daylight, ho!

ROMEO Nay that's not so.

MERCUTIO I mean sir, in delay   45

    We waste our lights in vain, like lamps by day.

    Take our good meaning, for our judgement sits

    Five times in that, ere once in our five wits.

ROMEO And we mean well in going to this mask;

    But 'tis no wit to go.   50

MERCUTIO Why, may one ask?

ROMEO I dreamt a dream tonight.

MERCUTIO And so did I.

ROMEO Well, what was yours?

MERCUTIO That dreamers often lie.   55

ROMEO In bed asleep while they do dream things true.

＊ MERCUTIO O then I see Queen Mab hath been with you.

BENVOLIO Queen Mab? What's she?

MERCUTIO She is the fairies' midwife, and she comes

    In shape no bigger than an agate stone   60

    On the forefinger of an alderman,

    Drawn with a team of little atomies

    Over men's noses as they lie asleep.

    Her chariot is an empty hazelnut,

Tickle the senseless floor with their heels.

I'll follow a grandfather's proverb:

I'll hold the candle and just look on;

Best to quit the game while it's still fun.

MERCUTIO Nonsense! As the sheriff says, be quiet as a mouse.   40

If you're a horse, we'll pull you from the muck—

Pardon me, I mean love—in which you're stuck

Up to your ears. Come, we're burning daylight.

ROMEO No, that's not true.

MERCUTIO I mean, sir, in this delay   45

We waste our time in vain, like lamps lit by day.

Take it as I mean it, for my meaning sits

In my words, not in the five senses.

ROMEO And we mean well in going to this feast,

But it's not wise to go.   50

MERCUTIO Why, may I ask?

ROMEO I dreamed a dream last night.

MERCUTIO And so did I.

ROMEO Well, what was yours?

MERCUTIO That dreamers often lie.   55

ROMEO In bed asleep while they dream things true.

MERCUTIO Oh, then, I see Queen Mab has been with you.

BENVOLIO Queen Mab? Who is she?

MERCUTIO She is the midwife fairy, and she comes

In size no bigger than an agate stone   60

On the forefinger of an alderman,

Drawn by a team of tiny creatures

Over men's noses as they lie asleep.

Her chariot is an empty hazelnut,

Made by the joiner squirrel or old grub, 65
Time out o' mind the fairies' coachmakers.
Her wagon-spokes made of long spinners' legs,
The cover the wings of grasshoppers,
Her traces of the smallest spider web,
Her collars of the moonshine's watery beams, 70
Her whip of cricket's bone; the lash, of film;
Her wagoner, a small grey-coated gnat,
Not half so big as a round little worm
Pricked from the lazy finger of a maid.
And in this state she gallops night by night 75
Through lovers' brains, and then they dream of love;
O'er courtiers' knees, that dream on curtsies straight;
O'er lawyers' fingers, who straight dream on fees;
O'er ladies' lips, who straight on kisses dream,
Which oft the angry Mab with blisters plagues, 80
Because their breaths with sweetmeats tainted are.
Sometime she gallops o'er a courtier's nose,
And then dreams he of smelling out a suit;
And sometime comes she with a tithe-pig's tail,
Tickling a parson's nose as 'a lies asleep, 85
Then dreams he of another benefice.
Sometimes she driveth o'er a soldier's neck,
And then dreams he of cutting foreign throats,
Of breaches, ambuscadoes, Spanish blades,
Of healths five fathom deep; and then anon 90
Drums in his ear, at which he starts and wakes,
And being thus frightened swears a prayer or two,
And sleeps again. This is that very Mab

Made by the carpenter squirrel, or maggot, 65

Longer than anyone can remember, the fairies' coachmakers.

Her wheel-spokes are made of long spiders' legs,

The coach top, of the wings of grasshoppers;

Her reins are of the smallest spiders' web;

Her collars, of the moonshine's watery beams; 70

Her whip, of cricket's bone; the lash, of silk.

Her coachman is a small grey-coated gnat,

Not half so big as a round little worm

Pricked from the finger of a lazy maid.

And in this splendor she gallops night after night 75

Through lovers' brains, and then they dream of love.

Over courtiers' knees, and they dream of bowing and scraping;

Over lawyers' fingers, and they dream of fees;

Over ladies' lips, and they dream of kisses,

Which often the testy Mab will plague with blisters, 80

Because their breaths smell of sweets.

Sometimes she gallops over a courtier's nose,

And then he dreams of finding a cause for a fee.

And sometimes she comes with a gift-pig's tail,

Tickling a parson's nose as he lies asleep, 85

Then he dreams of another well-paying post.

Sometimes she drives over a soldier's neck,

And then he dreams of cutting foreign throats,

Of breaching walls, ambushes, Spanish swords,

Of toasts drunk from glasses deep; and then, at once, 90

Drums he hears, at which he starts and wakes,

And being so frightened, he says a prayer or two,

And goes back to sleep. This is that same Mab

That plaits the manes of horses in the night,

And bakes the elf-locks in foul sluttish hairs, 95

Which once untangled much misfortune bodes.

This is the hag, when maids lie on their backs,

That presses them and learns them first to bear,

Making them women of good carriage.

This is she— 100

ROMEO Peace, peace, Mercutio, peace.

Thou talkest of nothing.

MERCUTIO True, I talk of dreams,

Which are the children of an idle brain,

Begot of nothing but vain fantasy, 105

Which is as thin of substance as the air

And more inconstant than the wind, who woos

Even now the frozen bosom of the north,

And, being anger'd, puffs away from thence,

Turning his face to the dew-dropping south. 110

BENVOLIO This wind you talk of blows us from ourselves.

Supper is done, and we shall come too late.

ROMEO I fear, too early; for my mind misgives

Some consequence, yet hanging in the stars,

Shall bitterly begin his fearful date 115

With this night's revels, and expire the term

Of a despised life closed in my breast

By some vile forfeit of untimely death.

But he that hath the steerage of my course

Direct my sail! On, lusty gentlemen! 120

BENVOLIO Strike, drum.

They march about the stage

Exeunt

44

Who braids the manes of horses in the night,

And mats the hair tangled by the elves,   95

Which, when untangled, foretells great misfortune.

This is the hag, when maids lie on their backs,

Who presses them, and teaches them first to bear,

Making them women of good carriage.

This is she—   100

ROMEO Stop, stop, Mercutio, stop,

You're talking nonsense.

MERCUTIO True, I talk of dreams,

Which are the children of an idle brain,

Born of nothing but idle fantasy   105

Which is as flimsy as the air

And less constant than the wind which blows

At first across the frozen wastes of the north

But then, growing angry, turns away

And moves to the milder southlands.   110

BENVOLIO This wind you talk of has blown us off course.

Supper will be over and we'll be too late.

ROMEO No, too early, for I sense

Some fearful event, planned by fate   > foreshadowing

Long ago will begin here tonight   115

At these festivities and with its

Malice end my unhappy life

With some horrible early death.

May God who guides my actions

Direct me now. Let's go enjoy ourselves!   120

BENVOLIO Strike, drummers!

They march about the stage

Exit

Scene 5 [*A hall in* CAPULET'S *house.* MUSICIANS *waiting*]

Enter SERVINGMEN *with napkins*

FIRST SERVANT Where's Potpan, that he helps not to take away? He shift a
trencher? He scrape a trencher?

SECOND SERVANT When good manners shall lie all in one or two men's
hands, and they unwashed too, 'tis a foul thing.

FIRST SERVANT Away with the joint stools, remove the court-   5
cupboard, look to the plate. Good thou, save me a piece
of marchpane, and, as thou loves me, let the porter let
in Susan Grindstone and Nell.

Exit SECOND SERVANT

Enter ANTHONY *and* POTPAN

Anthony and Potpan!

SECOND SERVANT Ay, boy, ready.   10

FIRST SERVANT You are looked for and called for, asked for and
sought for in the great chamber.

THIRD SERVANT We cannot be here and there too. Cheerly, boys,
be brisk a while, and the longer liver take all.

Exit SERVANTS

Enter CAPULET, *with* JULIET, TYBALT, *and others of his house,*
meeting the guests, ROMEO *and other* MASKERS

CAPULET Welcome gentlemen! Ladies that have their toes   15
Unplagued with corns will walk a bout with you.
Ah, my mistresses, which of you all
Will now deny to dance? She that makes dainty,
She, I'll swear, hath corns. Am I come near ye now?

Scene 5 [*A hall in* CAPULET'S house. MUSICIANS *waiting*]

Enter SERVINGMEN with napkins

FIRST SERVANT Where's Potpan who should be clearing the tables?

    He should be taking the plates away, not eating them clean.

SECOND SERVANT It's pretty bad when good service depends

    on one or two men, and they have dirty hands!

FIRST SERVANT Take away the stools and the sideboard, and the   5

    silverware. Be nice and save me a piece of almond candy.

    Then be a friend and tell the porter to let in Susan

    Grindstone and Nell.

Exit SECOND SERVANT

Enter ANTHONY and POTPAN

    Oh, Anthony and Potpan!

SECOND SERVANT Yes, I'll see to it all.   10

FIRST SERVANT Potpan, they've been looking and calling for you.

    They've asked and hunted for you in the ballroom.

THIRD SERVANT Well, we can't be here and there too. Cheer up,

    lads, work fast and the one who lasts longest gets the most.

Exit SERVANTS

Enter CAPULET with JULIET, T̃YBALT, and others of his house,

meeting the guests, ROMEO, and other MASKERS

CAPULET Welcome, gentlemen. Ladies whose toes are not   15

    In pain from corns will have a dance with you.

    Ah ha, my ladies! which of you all

    Will now decline to dance? She who refuses,

    She, I'll swear, has corns. Aren't I right?

Welcome gentlemen. I have seen the day   20

That I have worn a visor and could tell

A whispering tale in a fair lady's ear,

Such as would please. 'Tis gone, 'tis gone, 'tis gone,

You are welcome, gentlemen: come, musicians, play.

A hall, a hall, give room! And foot it girls!   25

Music plays and they dance

More light, you knaves, and turn the tables up.

And quench the fire, the room is grown too hot.

Ah sirrah, this unlooked-for sport comes well.

Nay sit, nay sit, good cousin Capulet,

For you and I are past our dancing days.   30

How long is't now since last yourself and I

Were in a mask?

COUSIN   By'r Lady, thirty years.

CAPULET   What, man, 'tis not so much, 'tis not so much.

'Tis since the nuptial of Lucentio,   35

Come Pentecost as quickly as it will,

Some five and twenty years, and then we masked.

COUSIN   'Tis more, 'tis more, his son is elder, sir;

His son is thirty.

CAPULET   Will you tell me that?   40

His son was but a ward two years ago.

ROMEO [*To a* SERVANT]   What lady's that which doth enrich the hand

Of yonder knight?

SERVANT   I know not sir.

ROMEO   O, she doth teach the torches to burn bright.   45

It seems she hangs upon the cheek of night

Welcome gentlemen. I have seen the day   20
When I have worn a mask, when I could tell
A whispering tale in a fair lady's ear—
One that would please her. But no more, no more, no more.
I welcome you gentlemen!
Come, musicians, play.   25
Clear the room for dancing. Now begin, girls.

The music plays, and they dance

Bring more light, waiters, and stack the tables up.
Put out the fire, the room is getting too hot.
Ah, friends, even these party crashers are welcome.
No, no, sit down, good cousin Capulet   30
For you and I are past our dancing days.
How long since you and I went masked to a dance?

COUSIN By Our Lady, thirty years.

CAPULET What, man, it can't be that long! Not that long!
Just since Lucentio's wedding,   35
At Pentecost, which comes soon.
It's twenty-five years since we went masked.

COUSIN No, more, even more. His son is older, sir,
His son is thirty!

CAPULET Can that be?
Surely he was a minor just two years ago.   40

ROMEO [*To a* SERVANT] Who is that graces the arm
Of the gentleman over there?

SERVANT I don't know, sir.

ROMEO Oh, she could teach light to burn bright. > sees Juliet 45
She seems to hang upon the cheek of night

As a rich jewel in an Ethiop's ear;
Beauty too rich for use, for earth too dear.
So shows a snowy dove trooping with crows
As yonder lady o'er her fellows shows. 50
The measure done, I'll watch her place of stand,
And touching hers, make blessed my rude hand.
Did my heart love till now? Foreswear it, sight.
For I ne'er saw true beauty till this night.
TYBALT This by his voice should be a Montague. 55
Fetch me my rapier, boy. What, dares the slave
Come hither, covered with an antic face
To fleer and scorn at our solemnity?
Now by the stock and honor of my kin,
To strike him dead I hold it not a sin. 60
CAPULET Why, how now, kinsman, wherefore storm you so?
TYBALT Uncle, this is a Montague, our foe:
A villain that is hither come in spite
To scorn at our solemnity this night.
CAPULET Young Romeo is it? 65
TYBALT 'Tis he, that villain Romeo.
CAPULET Content thee, gentle coz, let him alone.
'A bears him like a portly gentleman;
And, to say truth, Verona brags of him
To be a virtuous and well-governed youth. 70
I would not for the wealth of all this town
Here in my house do him disparagement.
Therefore, be patient, take no note of him.
It is my will, the which if thou respect,

Like a sparkling gem in a black lady's ear—
Beauty too rare for daily use, and too dear.
Among the other ladies she shows
Like a white dove among black crows.   50
The dance is done, so I'll see where she stands
And approaching, take her two hands.
Did I ever love till now? Admit it, sight,
I never saw true beauty till this night.

TYBALT I recognize that voice, it's young Montague.   55
 Boy, bring me my sword. Does this enemy
 Dare to come here masked
 To mock us at our own party?
 Well, in justice to my family honor and kin
 I must kill him, and I don't think that's a sin.   60

CAPULET What's wrong, Tybalt? What's upset you so?

TYBALT That man there's a Montague, our foe.
 A villain who has come here in spite
 To mock at our celebration tonight.

CAPULET Young Romeo, is it?   65

TYBALT Yes, it's that villain Romeo.

CAPULET Relax, young cousin, leave him alone.
 He's behaving like a gentleman
 And people speak well of him,
 Saying he's virtuous and courteous.   70
 I would not for the wealth of all this town
 Have him treated rudely in my house.
 Therefore, be patient, pay no attention to him.
 If you respect me, obey me.

Show a fair presence and put off these frowns, 75
An ill-beseeming semblance for a feast.

TYBALT It fits when such a villain is a guest:
I'll not endure him.

CAPULET He shall be endured.
What, goodman boy! I say he shall. Go to, 80
Am I the master here, or you? Go to.
You'll not endure him? God shall mend my soul,
You'll make a mutiny among my guests,
You will set cock-a-hoop, you'll be the man?

TYBALT Why, uncle, 'tis a shame. 85

CAPULET Go to, go to,
You are a saucy boy. Is't so indeed?
This trick may chance to scathe you, I know what.
You must contrary me. Marry, 'tis time.
Well said, my hearts!—you are a princox, go! 90
Be quiet, or—more light! more light!—For shame!
I'll make you quiet.—What, cheerly, my hearts!

TYBALT Patience perforce with wilful choler meeting
Makes my flesh tremble in their different greeting.
I will withdraw, but this intrusion shall, 95
Now seeming sweet, convert to bitterest gall.

Exit

ROMEO [*To* JULIET] If I profane with my unworthiest hand
This holy shrine, the gentle sin is this:
My lips, two blushing pilgrims, ready stand
To smooth that rough touch with a tender kiss. 100

JULIET Good pilgrim, you do wrong your hand too much,

Be good humored and don't frown. 75

It's out of place at a party.

TYBALT It fits, when such a villain is a guest—

I won't put up with him.

CAPULET Yes, you will!

Listen, young man, I say you will. Now, go away. 80

Am I the master here or you? Go away.

You won't put up with him? Bless my soul!

You'd start a noisy scene among my guests,

You'd turn my party into brawl, playing the big man?

TYBALT But uncle, it's a disgrace. 85

CAPULET No, go away.

You're a cocky lad, aren't you?

This behavior will harm you. I know that.

If you disobey me then it's time—

Oh, good dancing there, friends—you show-off, 90

Go away! Or stay but keep still. Bring more light!

For shame. I'll keep you quiet. Well danced, friends.

TYBALT Patience forced on me with obstinate ire

Makes me fearful of a resulting fire.

I will withdraw, but this intrusion will, 95

Now seeming sweet, become a bitter pill.

Exit TYBALT

ROMEO If I profane with my unworthy hand

This holy shrine, the only sin is this—

My lips, like blushing pilgrims, at ready stand

To smooth that rough touch with a tender kiss. 100

JULIET Good pilgrim, you do blame your hand too much,

Which mannerly devotion shows in this;

For saints have hands that pilgrims' hands do touch,

And palm to palm is holy palmers' kiss.

ROMEO Have not saints lips, and holy palmers too? 105

JULIET Ay, pilgrim, lips that they must use in prayer.

ROMEO O then, dear saint, let lips do what hands do!

They pray. Grant thou, lest faith turn to despair.

JULIET Saints do not move, though grant for prayer's sake.

ROMEO Then move not, while my prayer's effect I take. 110

[*He kisses her*]

Thus from my lips, by thine, my sin is purged.

JULIET Then have my lips the sin that they have took.

ROMEO Sin from my lips? O trespass sweetly urged!

Give me my sin again.

[*He kisses her again*]

JULIET You kiss by the book. 115

NURSE Madam, your mother craves a word with you.

ROMEO What is her mother?

NURSE Marry, bachelor,

Her mother is the lady of the house,

And a good lady, and a wise and virtuous. 120

I nursed her daughter that you talked withal.

I tell you, he that can lay hold of her

Shall have the chinks.

ROMEO Is she a Capulet?

O dear account! My life is my foe's debt. 125

BENVOLIO Away, be gone; the sport is at the best.

ROMEO Ay, so I fear; the more is my unrest.

CAPULET Nay, gentlemen, prepare not to be gone,

We have a trifling foolish banquet towards.

It only shows mannerly devotion in this;

For saints have hands that pilgrims' hands do touch

And palm to palm is holy palmers' kiss.

ROMEO Have not saints lips, and holy palmers too?   105

JULIET Yes, pilgrim, lips that they must use in prayer.

ROMEO Then, dear saint, let our lips do what hands do!

They pray, don't they, lest faith turn to despair.

JULIET Saints do not move except for prayer's sake.

ROMEO Then don't move while my prayer's answer take.   110

[*He kisses her*]

So that from my lips, by yours, my sin is purged.

JULIET Then my lips must now have the sin they took.

ROMEO Sin from my lips? An act that's sweetly urged!

Give me my sin again.

[*He kisses her again*]

JULIET You kiss by the book.   115

NURSE Madam, your mother craves a word with you.

ROMEO Who is her mother?

NURSE Why, young man,

Her mother is the lady of the house.

And she's a good lady, wise and virtuous.   120

I nursed her daughter whom you just talked to.

I'll tell you, whoever wins her heart

Will have plenty of money.

ROMEO Is she a Capulet?

Oh, costly game: I am in my enemy's debt.   125

BENVOLIO Let's go. The fun is over.

ROMEO Yes, so I fear, and the more is my unrest.

CAPULET Gentlemen, don't leave yet.

We'll have a little supper shortly.

[*They whisper in his ear*] Is it e'en so? Why then, I thank you all. 130

I thank you honest gentlemen, good night.

More torches here! Come on then, let's to bed.

Ah, sirrah, by my fay, it waxes late.

I'll to my rest.

Exeunt all but JULIET *and* NURSE

JULIET Come hither Nurse. What is yond gentleman?   135

NURSE The son and heir of old Tiberio.

JULIET What's he that now is going out of door?

NURSE Marry, that I think be young Petruchio.

JULIET What's he that follows here that would not dance?

NURSE I know not.   140

JULIET Go ask his name. If he be married,

My grave is like to be my wedding bed.

NURSE His name is Romeo, and a Montague,

The only son of your great enemy.

JULIET My only love sprung from my only hate!   145

Too early seen unknown, and known too late.

Prodigious birth of love it is to me

That I must love a loathed enemy.

NURSE What's this? What's this?

JULIET A rhyme I learned even now   150

Of one I danced withal. [*One calls within* "Juliet!"]

NURSE Anon, anon!

Come, let's away. The strangers are all gone.

Exeunt

[*They whisper in his ear.*] Is that so? Why then, I thank you all. 130

I thank you, honest gentlemen. Good night.

Bring some light over here. It's time for bed.

Oh, my, it has gotten late.

I'll go to bed now.

Exit all but JULIET *and* NURSE

JULIET Come here, Nurse. Who is that young gentleman? 135

NURSE The son and heir of old Tiberio.

JULIET And the one just going out the door?

NURSE Why, I think that's young Petruchio.

JULIET What about the one following, who would not dance?

NURSE I don't know. 140

JULIET Go ask his name, and if he is married,

My wedding bed will likely be my grave.

NURSE His name's Romeo. He's a Montague.

The only son of your great enemy.

JULIET The one I love the son of the one I hate. 145

When we met I didn't know, and now it's too late.

How unlucky in love for me

To find I love my enemy.

NURSE What's that? What's that?

JULIET A rhyme I learned just now 150

From someone I danced with. [*One calls within* "Juliet"]

NURSE Right away! Right away!

But come, let's go. The guests have all gone.

Exit

PROLOGUE

Enter CHORUS

Now old desire doth in his deathbed lie,

    And young affection gapes to be his heir;

That fair for which love groaned for and would die,

    With tender Juliet matched, is now not fair.

Now Romeo is beloved, and loves again,   5

    Alike bewitched by the charm of looks;

But to his foe supposed he must complain,

    And she steal love's sweet bait from fearful hooks.

Being held a foe, he may not have access

    To breathe such vows as lovers use to swear;   10

And she, as much in love, her means much less

    To meet her new beloved anywhere.

But passion lends them power, time means to meet,

Tempering extremities with extreme sweet.

                          Exeunt

PROLOGUE

Enter SPEAKER

The old love does now on its deathbed lie,
    And new desire longs to be its heir;
That fair maid, whom love sighed for, and would die,
    Compared to Juliet, she is now not fair.
Now Romeo is beloved, and loves again,   5
    Both alike are bewitched by charming looks.
But to his supposed foe he must explain,
    And she steal love's sweet bait from fearful hooks.
Being a foe, he cannot have access
    To breathe such vows as lovers make and swear;   10
And she, as much in love, has even less
    A chance to meet her new love anywhere.
But passion gives them power and time the means to meet,
Tempering woes with things extremely sweet.

                        Exit

Act Two

Scene 1 [*A lane by the wall of Capulet's orchard*]

Enter ROMEO

ROMEO Can I go forward when my heart is here?

Turn back, dull earth, and find thy center out.

[*He withdraws*]

Enter BENVOLIO *and* MERCUTIO

BENVOLIO Romeo! My cousin Romeo! Romeo!

MERCUTIO He is wise,

And on my life, hath stolen him home to bed.   5

BENVOLIO He ran this way, and leapt this orchard wall.

Call, good Mercutio.

MERCUTIO Nay, I'll conjure too.

Romeo! Humors! Madman! Passion! Lover!

Appear thou in the likeness of a sigh,   10

Speak but one rhyme and I am satisfied.

Cry but "Ay, me!" Pronounce but "love" and "dove,"

Speak to my gossip Venus one fair word,

One nickname for her purblind son and heir,

Young Adam Cupid, he that shot so trim   15

When King Cophetua loved the beggar maid.

He heareth not, he stirreth not, he moveth not!

The ape is dead, and I must conjure him.

I conjure thee by Rosaline's bright eyes,

By her high forehead and her scarlet lip,   20

By her fine foot, straight leg, and quivering thigh,

And the demesnes that there adjacent lie,

That in thy likeness thou appear to us!

Act Two

Scene 1 [*A lane by the wall of Capulet's orchard*]

Enter ROMEO

ROMEO How can I walk on, now that my heart is here?

Turn back, dull clod, and find the center of your world.

[*He withdraws*]

Enter BENVOLIO *and* MERCUTIO

BENVOLIO Romeo! My cousin Romeo! Romeo!

MERCUTIO He is wise.

I am willing to bet he's stolen home to bed.   5

BENVOLIO He ran this way and climbed this orchard wall.

Call him, good Mercutio.

MERCUTIO No, I'll say the magic words:

Romeo, moody madman, passionate lover!

Appear now in the likeness of a sigh.   10

Speak just one rhyme, and I'll be satisfied.

Cry just one "I'm here," pronounce just one "love" and "dove";

Speak to my friend Venus just one kind word,

One nickname for her blindfolded son and heir,

Young Adam Cupid, who shot so true   15

He caused a king to love a beggar maid.

He must not hear us, he has not stirred, he has not moved.

He's playing possum, but I'll rouse him.

I call upon you by Rosaline's bright eyes,

By her high forehead and her scarlet lips,   20

By her dainty feet, straight legs and quivering thighs,

And by all the surrounding areas.

Come out of hiding and appear as yourself.

BENVOLIO And if he hear thee, thou wilt anger him.

MERCUTIO This cannot anger him. 'Twould anger him   25
    To raise a spirit in his mistress' circle
    Of some strange nature, letting it there stand
    Till she had laid it and conjured it down;
    That were some spite. My invocation
    Is fair and honest: in his mistress' name,   30
    I conjure only but to raise up him.

BENVOLIO Come, he hath hid himself among these trees
    To be consorted with the humorous night.
    Blind is his love, and best befits the dark.

MERCUTIO If love be blind, love cannot hit the mark.   35
    Now will he sit under a medlar tree
    And wish his mistress were that kind of fruit
    As maids call medlars when they laugh alone.
    O Romeo, that she were, O that she were
    An open, and thou a poperin pear!   40
    Romeo, good night. I'll to my truckle-bed.
    This field-bed is too cold for me to sleep.
    Come, shall we go?

BENVOLIO Go then, for 'tis in vain
    To seek him here that means not to be found.   45

Exeunt BENVOLIO *and* MERCUTIO

BENVOLIO And if he hears you, you will anger him.

MERCUTIO This cannot anger him. It would anger him   25
  If I raised a spirit in his beloved's presence,
  Some strange spirit that stood there
  Until she cast a spell to remove it.
  Now that would be spiteful, but my conjuring
  Is fair and honest: in his beloved's name,   30
  I conjured only but to raise him up.

BENVOLIO Come, he has hid himself among these trees
  To be alone in the damp and dewy night.
  His love is blind, so it suits the dark.

MERCUTIO But if love is blind, it cannot hit the mark.   35
  Now he'll sit under an apple tree
  And wish his beloved were that kind of fruit
  Girls call "apples" when they joke in private.
  Oh, Romeo, if she were, if only she were
  A ripe apple and you a long, thick pear.   40
  Good night Romeo. I'm off to my trundle bed.
  This field's too cold for me to sleep in.
  Come, shall we go?

BENVOLIO Let us go. It is useless to look
  For one who refuses to be found.   45

  Exit BENVOLIO *and* MERCUTIO

Scene 2 [*Capulet's Orchard*]

ROMEO *comes forward*

✳ ROMEO He jests at scars that never felt a wound.

[*An upper window lights up*]

But soft, what light through yonder window breaks?

It is the east and Juliet is the sun! ⟩ metaphor

Arise fair sun and kill the envious moon

Who is already sick and pale with grief,   ⟩ know   5

That thou her maid art far more fair than she.   who said!

Be not her maid since she is envious,

Her vestal livery is but sick and green

And none but fools do wear it. Cast it off.

Enter JULIET *above*

It is my lady, O it is my love!   10

O that she knew she were!

She speaks, yet she says nothing. What of that?

Her eye discourses. I will answer it.

I am too bold. 'Tis not to me she speaks.

Two of the fairest stars in all the heaven,   15

Having some business, do entreat her eyes

To twinkle in their spheres till they return.

What if her eyes were there, they in her head?

The brightness of her cheek would shame those stars

As daylight doth a lamp. Her eyes in heaven   20

Would through the airy region stream so bright

That birds would sing and think it were not night.

See how she leans her cheek upon her hand.

Scene 2 [*Capulet's Orchard*]

ROMEO *comes forward*

ROMEO He jests at scars that never felt a wound.

[*An upper window lights up*]

But wait, what light through yonder window breaks?

It must be the east, and Juliet is the sun!

Arise fair sun and kill the envious moon

Who is already sick and pale with grief   5

That you, her handmaid, are far more fair than she.

Don't be her maid, since she is envious.

Her virgin dress is pale and green for lack of love,

And only fools wear that. Throw it off.

Enter JULIET *above*

It is my lady there; it is my love!   10

If only she knew that she were!

She speaks, yet she says nothing. What of that?

Her eyes can speak. I'll answer them.

I'm too hasty. It's not to me she speaks.

Two of the fairest stars in all the heavens,   15

Having business elsewhere, beg her eyes

To take their place till they return.

What if they did change places?

The brightness of her face would shame those stars,

As sunlight puts a lamp to shame. Her eyes in heaven   20

Would shine through skies and clouds so bright

That birds would sing and think it were not night.

See how she leans her cheek upon her hand!

compares her to celestial bodies & an angel.

O that I were a glove upon that hand,

That I might touch that cheek! 25

JULIET Ay me!

ROMEO She speaks.

O speak again bright angel, for thou art

As glorious to this night, being o'er my head,

As is a winged messenger of heaven 30

Unto the white-upturned wondering eyes

Of mortals that fall back to gaze on him

When he bestrides the lazy-pacing clouds

And sails upon the bosom of the air.

*JULIET O Romeo, Romeo, wherefore art thou Romeo? 35

Deny thy father and refuse thy name.

Or if thou wilt not, be but sworn my love,

And I'll no longer be a Capulet.

> know who said!

ROMEO Shall I hear more, or shall I speak at this?

JULIET 'Tis but thy name that is my enemy; 40

Thou art thyself, though not a Montague.

What's Montague? It is nor hand nor foot

Nor arm nor face nor any other part

Belonging to a man. O be some other name.

What's in a name? That which we call a rose 45

By any other word would smell as sweet.

So Romeo would, were he not Romeo called,

Retain that dear perfection which he owes

Without that title. Romeo, doff thy name,

And for that name, which is no part of thee, 50

Take all myself.

I wish I were a glove upon that hand
So I might touch her cheek. 25

JULIET Oh dear.

ROMEO She speaks.

Oh, speak again, <u>bright angel</u>! for you are
As glorious in this night, so high above me,
As is <u>a winged angel sent from heaven</u> 30
To the upturned, wondering eyes
Of mortals who bend back to gaze on him
As he rides the lazy-pacing clouds
And sails on through the air.

JULIET Oh, Romeo, Romeo! Why must you be "Romeo"? 35

Disown your father and refuse your name.
Or if you won't, just swear your love
And I'll no longer be a Capulet.

> shows she's
serious about
loving him

ROMEO Should I listen to more, or should I speak out now?

JULIET It's only your name that is my enemy. 40
You'd be you, whatever your name.
What's a Montague? It is not a hand or foot
Or arm, or face, or any other part
Belonging to a man. Oh, take some other name.
<u>What's in a name? What we call a rose</u> 45
<u>Would by any other name smell as sweet.</u>
<u>So would Romeo, if he were not named Romeo,</u>
<u>Still have that dear perfection that he owns</u>
<u>Without that name. Romeo, give up that name</u>
<u>And in exchange for it, which is no part of you,</u> 50
<u>Take all of me.</u>

ROMEO I take thee at thy word.

    Call me but "love," and I'll be new baptized:

    Henceforth I never will be Romeo.

JULIET What man art thou that thus bescreened in night   55

    So stumblest on my counsel?

ROMEO By a name

    I know not how to tell thee who I am:

    My name, dear saint, is hateful to myself

    Because it is an enemy to thee.   60

    Had I it written, I would tear the word.

JULIET My ears have not drunk a hundred words

    Of thy tongue's uttering, yet I know the sound.

    Art thou not Romeo, and a Montague?

ROMEO Neither, fair maid, if either thee dislike.   65

JULIET How cam'st thou hither, tell me, and wherefore?

    The orchard walls are high and hard to climb,

    And the place death, considering who thou art,

    If any of my kinsmen find thee here.

ROMEO With love's light wings did I o'erperch these walls,   70

    For stony limits cannot hold love out,

    And what love can do, that dares love attempt:

    Therefore thy kinsmen are no stop to me.

JULIET If they do see thee, they will murder thee.

ROMEO Alack, there lies more peril in thine eye   75

    Than twenty of their swords. Look thou but sweet

    And I am proof against their enmity.

JULIET I would not for the world they saw thee here.

ROMEO I have night's cloak to hide me from their eyes,

ROMEO I'll take you at your word.

    Just call me "love," and I'll be rechristened.

    Henceforth, I never will be Romeo.

JULIET Who are you, there screened in the dark,   55

    And listening in on my secrets?

ROMEO If I have to use a name,

    I don't know how to tell you who I am:

    My name, dear saint, is hateful to me

    Because it is an enemy to you.   60

    If it were written down, I'd tear it up.

JULIET My ears have not drunk a hundred words

    Your tongue has spoken, but I know your voice.

    Aren't you Romeo and a Montague?

ROMEO Neither, lovely one, if either you dislike.   65

JULIET How did you get in here, please tell me, and why?

    The orchard walls are high and hard to climb,

    And this place is death, considering who you are,

    If any of my kinsmen find you here.

ROMEO Love gave me wings to fly with;   70

    For walls of stone cannot keep love out.

    And what love can do, he who loves, dares.

    Therefore your kinsmen are no hurdle to me.

JULIET If they see you here, they will murder you.

ROMEO Perhaps so, but there's more danger in your eyes   75

    Than from twenty of their swords. Just sweetly smile,

    And I'm safe from their hatred.

JULIET I would not for the world they saw you here.

ROMEO I have the cloak of night to hide me from their eyes;

And but thou love me, let them find me here. 80

My life were better ended by their hate

Than death prorogued, wanting of thy love.

JULIET By whose direction found'st thou out this place?

ROMEO By love, that first did prompt me to inquire.

He lent me counsel, and I lent him eyes. 85

I am no pilot, yet wert thou as far

As that vast shore washed with the farthest sea,

I should adventure for such merchandise.

JULIET Thou knowest the mask of night is on my face

Else would a maiden blush bepaint my cheek 90

For that which thou hast heard me speak tonight.

Fain would I dwell on form; fain, fain deny

What I have spoke. But farewell compliment!

Dost thou love me? I know thou wilt say "Ay,"

And I will take thy word. Yet if thou swearest, 95

Thou may'st prove false. At lovers' perjuries,

They say, Jove laughs. O gentle Romeo,

If thou dost love, pronounce it faithfully.

Or, if thou think'st I am too quickly won,

I'll frown and be perverse and say thee nay, 100

So thou wilt woo; but else, not for the world.

In truth, fair Montague, I am too fond,

And therefore thou may'st think my 'haviour light,

But trust me, gentleman, I'll prove more true

Than those that have more cunning to be strange. 105

I should have been more strange, I must confess,

But that thou overheard'st, ere I was ware,

But if you don't love me, let them find me here.   80

Better my life be ended by their hate

Than death delayed, lacking your love.

JULIET At whose direction did you find this place?

ROMEO By love, which first prompted me to inquire.

Love gave me counsel, and I gave him eyes.   85

Although I'm no pilot, still, if you were

As far as the farthest shore washed by the sea,

I'd risk everything for such a reward.

JULIET You know the dark of night masks my face,

Or you'd see a blush upon my cheek   90

For that which you heard me say tonight.

Gladly, I would stand on form; gladly, gladly deny

What I have said. But goodbye to being proper.

Do you love me? I know you'll say "yes,"

And I'll take your word. Yet you might swear   95

And still prove false. They say the gods laugh

At lovers' lies. Oh, gentle Romeo,

If you really love me, swear it truly.

But if you think I'm too easily won,

I'll scowl and spurn you, and I'll tell you "no,"   100

To keep you guessing, though not for any other reason.

To be honest, fair Montague, I'm so in love,

That you must think me unladylike.

But trust me, gentleman, I'll prove more true

Than women who play hard to get.   105

I should have been more distant, I admit,

But you heard me confessing my love

My true-love passion; therefore pardon me,

And not impute this yielding to light love.

Which the dark night hath so discovered. 110

ROMEO Lady, by yonder blessed moon I vow,

That tips with silver all these fruit-tree tops—

JULIET O swear not by the moon, th' inconstant moon,

That monthly changes in her circled orb,

Lest that thy love prove likewise variable. 115

ROMEO What shall I swear by?

JULIET Do not swear at all.

Or, if thou wilt, swear by thy gracious self,

Which is the god of my idolatry,

And I'll believe thee. 120

ROMEO If my heart's dear love—

JULIET Well, do not swear. Although I joy in thee,

I have no joy of this contract tonight:

It is too rash, too unadvised, too sudden,

Too like the lightning, which doth cease to be 125

Ere one can say "It lightens." Sweet, good night.

This bud of love, by summer's ripening breath,

May prove a beauteous flower when next we meet.

Good night, and good night! As sweet repose and rest

Come to thy heart as that within my breast. 130

ROMEO O wilt thou leave me so unsatisfied?

JULIET What satisfaction canst thou have tonight?

ROMEO The exchange of thy love's faithful vow for mine.

JULIET I gave thee mine before thou didst request it,

And yet I would it were to give again. 135

Before I knew you were there. Please, forgive me,

And don't think my yielding quickly means a loose love,

Which the dark night has brought to light. 110

ROMEO Lady, I swear by the distant blessed moon

That gilds with silver all these fruit-tree tops—

JULIET Oh, don't swear by the changeable moon

That each month moves from full to thin,

In case your love changes too. 115

ROMEO What shall I swear by?

JULIET Do not swear at all.

Or, if you must, swear by your sweet self,

Which I do worship,

And I'll believe you. 120

ROMEO If my heart's dear love—

JULIET Well, do not swear. Although you give me joy,

I get no joy from this exchange of vows tonight.

It is too rash, too ill-advised, too sudden,

Too like lightening that is over before 125

You can say "Look!" Good night, dear.

This bud of love, ripened by summer's breath,

May prove a beautiful flower when next we meet.   *> beleivs new love will blossom*

Good night, good night! May as sweet a sleep and rest

Come to your heart as that within my breast. 130

ROMEO Oh, will you leave me so unsatisfied?

JULIET What satisfaction can you have tonight?

ROMEO The exchange of your love's faithful vow for mine.

JULIET I gave you mine even before you asked for it.

And yet I wish I could take it back. 135

ROMEO Wouldst thou withdraw it? For what purpose, love?

JULIET But to be frank and give it thee again;

And yet I wish but for the thing I have.

My bounty is as boundless as the sea,

My love as deep; the more I give to thee   140

The more I have, for both are infinite.

[NURSE *calls within*]

I hear some noise within. Dear love, adieu.

Anon, good Nurse! Sweet Montague be true.

Stay but a little, I will come again.

Exit JULIET

ROMEO O blessed, blessed night. I am afeard,   145

Being in night, all this is but a dream,

Too flattering sweet to be substantial.

Enter JULIET *above*

JULIET Three words, dear Romeo, and good night indeed.

If that thy bent of love be honorable,

Thy purpose marriage, send me word tomorrow   150

By one that I'll procure to come to thee,

Where and what time thou wilt perform the rite,

And all my fortunes at thy foot I'll lay,

And follow thee my lord throughout the world.

NURSE [*Within*] Madam!   155

JULIET I come, anon—But if thou meanest not well

I do beseech thee—

NURSE [*Within*] Madam!

JULIET By and by I come—

To cease thy strife and leave me to my grief.   160

Handwritten margin note: compares her love to a rose & the sea

ROMEO Would you withdraw it? For what reason, love?

JULIET Just so I could give it again.

But I'm asking for what I still have.

My capacity to give is as boundless as the sea,

My love as deep, and the more I give to you   140

The more I have, for both are infinite.

[NURSE *calls within*]

Someone is calling. Dear love, adieu.

In a moment, Nurse. Sweet Montague, be true.

Wait here. I'll come back.

Exit JULIET

ROMEO Oh blessed, blessed night! But I'm afraid,   145

Because it is night, all this is but a dream,

Too deceptively sweet to be real.

Enter JULIET *above*

JULIET Just three words, dear Romeo, and then good night, indeed.

If the intention of your love is honorable,

Your object marriage, send me word tomorrow,   150

By someone I'll engage to come to you,

Where and when the ceremony will be.

Then all my future at your feet I'll lay,

And follow you, my husband, throughout the world.

NURSE [*Within*] Mistress!   155

JULIET I'm coming. But if you aren't sincere,

Then I beg you—

NURSE [*Within*] Mistress!

JULIET I'll be there—

To pursue me no more and leave me to my sorrow.   160

[handwritten note: To prove he loves her she says he must marry her.]

75

Tomorrow will I send.

ROMEO So thrive my soul—

JULIET A thousand times good night.

Exit JULIET

ROMEO A thousand times the worse, to want thy light.

    Love goes toward love as schoolboys from their books,   165

    But love from love, toward school with heavy looks.

Enter JULIET again above

JULIET Hist! Romeo, hist! O for a falconer's voice

    To lure this tassel-gentle back again.

    Bondage is hoarse and may not speak aloud.

    Else would I tear the cave where Echo lies   170

    And make her airy tongue more hoarse than mine

    With repetition of my "Romeo."

ROMEO It is my soul that calls upon my name.

    How silver-sweet sound lovers' tongues by night,

    Like softest music to attending ears.   175

JULIET Romeo!

ROMEO My dear?

JULIET What o'clock tomorrow

    Shall I send to thee?

ROMEO By the hour of nine.   180

JULIET I will not fail. 'Tis twenty year till then.

    I have forgot why I did call thee back.

ROMEO Let me stand here till thou remember it.

JULIET I shall forget, to have thee still stand there,

    Remembering how I love thy company.   185

ROMEO And I'll still stay, to have thee still forget,

    Forgetting any other home but this.

Until tomorrow then.

ROMEO By my everlasting soul, I—

JULIET A thousand times good night.

Exit JULIET

ROMEO A thousand times worse to lack your light.

    Love runs toward love as schoolboys run from books;   165

    But love leaves love as they return with heavy looks.

Enter JULIET again, above

JULIET Psst! Romeo! Psst! Oh, for a falconer's voice

    To lure this noble hawk back again.

    I am not free right now to speak out loud,

    Or I would tear the air of Echo's cave   170

    And make her airy voice more hoarse than mine

    With repetition of my "Romeo."

ROMEO It is my love that calls me by my name.

    How silvery-sweet lovers' voices sound at night,

    Like the softest music to our listening ears.   175

JULIET Romeo!

ROMEO My sweet.

JULIET At what time tomorrow

    Shall I send the messenger?

ROMEO By nine o'clock.   180

JULIET I will not fail. It's twenty years till then.

    I've forgotten why I called you back.

ROMEO Let me stand here till you remember it.

JULIET I will forget, just to keep you here,

    Remembering how I love your company.   185

ROMEO And I'll stay still so you'll keep forgetting.

    I've forgotten any home but this.

JULIET 'Tis almost morning. I would have thee gone;

    And yet no farther than a wanton's bird,

    That lets it hop a little from her hand,   190

    Like a poor prisoner in his twisted gyves,

    And with a silk thread plucks it back again,

    So loving-jealous of his liberty.

ROMEO I would I were thy bird.

JULIET Sweet, so would I.   195

    Yet I should kill thee with much cherishing.

    Good night, good night! Parting is such sweet sorrow

    That I shall say "good night" till it be morrow.

                   Exit

ROMEO Sleep dwell upon thine eyes, peace in thy breast!

    Would I were sleep and peace, so sweet to rest!   200

    Hence will I to my ghostly friar's close cell,

    His help to crave and my dear hap to tell.

                   Exit

Scene 3 [*Friar Lawrence's cell*]

          Enter FRIAR LAWRENCE *with a basket*

FRIAR LAWRENCE The grey-eyed morn smiles on the frowning

    night.

    Check'ring the eastern clouds with streaks of light;

    And fleckled darkness like a drunkard reels

    From forth day's path and Titan's fiery wheels.   5

[Handwritten note: Soliloquy: long speech that reveals the thoughts & feelings of a character who is alone on stage.]

JULIET It's almost morning; I think you should go,

    But no farther than a spoiled child's bird,

    Allowed to hop a little from her hand,   190

    But then like a prisoner in chains,

    Is pulled back again by silken threads

    Because she cannot part with it.

ROMEO I wish I were that bird.

JULIET Sweetheart, so do I.   195

    But I'd smother you with too much loving.

    Good night, good night! Parting is such sweet sorrow

    That I shall say "good night" till it be morrow.

Exit JULIET

ROMEO Sleep dwell upon your eyes, peace in your breast.

    I wish I were sleep and peace, how sweet I'd rest.   200

    I'll go now to my priest to confess,

    To ask his help, and to share my happiness.

Exit ROMEO

Scene 3 [*Friar Lawrence's cell*]

Enter FRIAR LAWRENCE *with a basket*

FRIAR LAWRENCE The grey-eyed dawn smiles on the frowning

    <u>night,</u>   > personification

    Checkering the eastern clouds with streaks of light.

    And speckled darkness, like a drunkard, reels

    From out of the sun's way and his chariot wheels.   5

Lawrence's attributes: seems like a hope full person, educated, deep thinker, insightful

Now, ere the sun advance his burning eye ⟩ personification
The day to cheer, and night's dank dew to dry,
I must up-fill this osier cage of ours
With baleful weeds and precious-juiced flowers.
The earth that's nature's mother is her tomb; ⟩ personification   10
What is her burying grave, that is her womb.
And from her womb children of divers kind
We sucking on her natural bosom find;
Many for many virtues excellent,
None but for some, and yet all different.   15
O, mickle is the powerful grace that lies
In plants, herb, stones, and their true qualities;
For nought so vile that on the earth doth live
But to the earth some special good doth give;
Nor aught so good but, strained from that fair use;   20
Revolts from true birth, stumbling on abuse;
Virtue itself turns vice, being misapplied,
And vice sometime's by action dignified.

Enter ROMEO

Within the infant rind of this weak flower
Poison hath residence, and medicine power,   ⟩ don't judge by looks   25
For this, being smelt, with that part cheers each part;
Being tasted, stays all sense with the heart.
Two such opposed kings encamp them still
In man as well as herbs—grace and rude will;   ⟩ both good and bad can exsist in people & plants   30
And where the worser is predominant,
Full soon the canker death eats up that plant.
ROMEO Good morrow father!

Now, before the sun advances in the sky,

To cheer the day and cause night's dank dew to dry,

I must fill up this wicker basket of ours

With deadly weeds and precious, healing flowers.

> he must do before sunrise; their healing powers

The earth is nature's mother and her tomb;

The grave of earth serves also as her womb.

And from her womb children of all kind

Nurse and are nourished for us to find.

Many have healing powers;

Others are just pretty flowers.   15

Oh, wondrous is the powerful grace that lies

In plants, herbs, stones, and their true qualities.

For even vile things that on earth do live

Back to the earth some special good can give.

But even good plants, if departing from good use,   20

Can be made evil by someone's abuse.

Virtue itself turns vice, if misapplied,

And vice sometimes by action is dignified.

Enter ROMEO

Within the seeds of this delicate flower

Poison can reside and also healing power.   25

There is a sweet fragrance in this part

But in that a taste that stops the heart.

In men, as well as in herb's core,

Two opposing powers may war.

And where the worser is predominant   30

Quite soon the worm, death, eats that plant.

ROMEO   Good morning, Father.

FRIAR LAWRENCE   Benedicite!

    What early tongue so sweet saluteth me?

    Young son, it argues a distempered head   35

    So soon to bid good morrow to thy bed.

    Care keeps his watch in every old man's eye,

    And where care lodges sleep will never lie;

    But where unbruised youth with unstuffed brain

    Doth couch his limbs, there golden sleep doth reign.   40

    Therefore thy earliness doth me assure

    Thou art uproused with some distemperature;

    Or if not so, then here I hit it right:

    Our Romeo hath not been in bed tonight.

ROMEO   That last is true. The sweeter rest was mine.   45

FRIAR LAWRENCE   God pardon sin! Wast thou with Rosaline?

ROMEO   With Rosaline, my ghostly father? No.

    I have forgot that name, and that name's woe.

FRIAR LAWRENCE   That's my good son; but where hast thou

        been then?   50

ROMEO   I'll tell thee ere thou ask it me again.

    I have been feasting with mine enemy.

    Where, on a sudden, one hath wounded me

    That's by me wounded. Both our remedies

    Within thy help and holy physic lies.   55

    I bear no hatred, blessed man, for lo,

    My intercession likewise steads my foe.

FRIAR LAWRENCE   Be plain, good son, and homely in thy drift.

    Riddling confession but riddling shrift.

ROMEO   Then plainly know my heart's dear love is set   60

FRIAR LAWRENCE Benedicite.

    Whose early voice so pleasantly greets me?

    Young man, it seems as if an aching head   35

    Has driven you too soon from your bed.

    Worry can disturb an old man's head

    And while he worries, sleep has fled.

    But a young man should have a clear mind

    And when he rests, golden sleep is kind.   40

    Therefore your earliness makes me feel assured

    You are upset about something you want cured.

    Or else I bet I can guess right:

    Our Romeo has not been to bed tonight.

ROMEO Yes, you're right, but sweeter rest was mine.   45

FRIAR LAWRENCE God pardon sin! Were you with Rosaline?

ROMEO With Rosaline, my holy father?

    I have forgotten her name and all that bother.

FRIAR LAWRENCE That's good, my son! But where were

        you then?   50

ROMEO I'll tell you lest you ask me once again.

    I had been feasting with my enemy,

    When suddenly someone captured me

    And I captured her. Now our remedies

    Within your help and holy powers lie.   55

    I bear no hatred, blessed man, no;

    For my request also aids my foe.

FRIAR LAWRENCE Speak plainer, good son, help me in my confusion.

    A puzzling confession gets only partial absolution.

ROMEO Then plainly know my heart's dear love is set   60

On the fair daughter of rich Capulet.

As mine on hers, so hers is set on mine;

And all combined, saved what thou must combine

By holy marriage. When, and where, and how,

We met, we wooed, and made exchange of vow, 65

I'll tell thee as we pass; but this I pray,

That thou consent to marry us today.

FRIAR LAWRENCE Holy Saint Francis! What a change is here!

Is Rosaline, that thou didst love so dear,

So soon forsaken? Young man's love, then, lies 70

Not truly in their hearts, but in their eyes.

> he is concerned about Romeo

Jesu Maria, what a deal of brine

Hath washed thy sallow cheeks for Rosaline!

How much salt water thrown away in waste,

To season love, that of it doth not taste! 75

The sun not yet thy sighs from heaven clears,

Thy old groans yet ring in mine ancient ears;

Lo, here upon thy cheek the stain doth sit

Of an old tear that is not washed off yet.

If e'er thou wast thyself, and these woes thine, 80

Thou and these woes were all for Rosaline.

And art thou changed? Pronounce this sentence, then:

Women may fall, when there's no strength in men.

ROMEO Thou chid'st me oft for loving Rosaline.

FRIAR LAWRENCE For doting, not for loving, pupil mine. 85

ROMEO And bad'st me bury love.

FRIAR LAWRENCE Not in a grave,

To lay one in, another out to have.

On the fair daughter of rich Capulet.

As mine on hers, so hers is set on mine.

All else united, now you must combine

By holy marriage our two souls. When and how

We met, we wooed, and exchanged a vow,   65

I'll tell you as we walk. But this I pray,

That you consent to marry us today.

FRIAR LAWRENCE Holy St. Francis! What a change is here!

Is Rosaline that you did love so dear

So soon forgotten? Young men's love then lies   70

Not truly in their hearts but in their eyes.

Dear God, what a lot of brine

Flowed down your cheeks for Rosaline!

How many torrents of salt water did fall

To flavor love that wasn't love at all?   75

The sun not yet your sighs from heaven clears;

Your old groans still ring in my old man's ears.

Look here, upon your cheek the stains still sit

Of old tears that are not washed off yet.

If you were sincere in your woe,   80

It was all for Rosaline, so

Are you now changed? Say this after me:

Women are faithless when men so weak can be.

ROMEO You often scolded me for loving Rosaline.

FRIAR LAWRENCE For infatuation, not love, pupil mine.   85

ROMEO And told me to bury love.

FRIAR LAWRENCE Not in a grave, just so

You could take another. No!

ROMEO I pray thee chide me not. Her I love now

    Doth grace for grace and for love allow;   90

    The other did not so.

FRIAR LAWRENCE O, she knew well

    Thy love did read by rote that could not spell.

    But come, young waverer, come, go with me,

    In one respect I'll thy assistant be;   95

    For this alliance may so happy prove

    To turn your households' rancor to pure love.

ROMEO O, let us hence; I stand on sudden haste.

FRIAR LAWRENCE Wisely and slow; they stumble that run fast. > take it easy!

                                 Exeunt

Scene 4 [*A street, later that morning*]

               Enter BENVOLIO *and* MERCUTIO

MERCUTIO Where the devil should this Romeo be?

    Came he not home tonight?

BENVOLIO Not to his father's. I spoke with his man.

MERCUTIO Why, that same pale hard-hearted wench, that

    Rosaline, torments him so that he will sure run mad.   5

BENVOLIO Tybalt, the kinsman to old Capulet, hath sent a

    letter to his father's house.

MERCUTIO A challenge, on my life.

BENVOLIO Romeo will answer it.

MERCUTIO Any man that can write may answer a letter.   10

BENVOLIO Nay, he will answer the letter's master, how he

ROMEO Please don't scold me. The one I now love

Cares for me and with her love returns my love.   90

Rosaline did not.

FRIAR LAWRENCE Oh, she must have seen

You were reciting words you didn't mean.

Well, young man, come with me.

In one thing I'll your assistant be.   95

For this alliance may happily prove

To end your families' feud, their hate remove.

> Thinks it will end feud between the two households.

ROMEO Please, let's go! My patience will not last.

FRIAR LAWRENCE Wisely and slow; they stumble who run fast.

Exit

Scene 4 [*A Street, later that morning*] *nurse meets Romeo*

Enter BENVOLIO *and* MERCUTIO

MERCUTIO Where the devil can Romeo be?

Didn't he come home last night?

BENVOLIO Not to his father's. I asked his servant.

MERCUTIO Why that pale-faced, hard-hearted flirt Rosaline

will drive him crazy with her rejection.   5

BENVOLIO Tybalt, the kinsman to old Capulet, has sent Romeo

a letter at his father's house.

MERCUTIO A challenge to a duel, as sure as I'm alive.

BENVOLIO Romeo will answer it.

MERCUTIO Anyone who can write, can answer a letter.   10

BENVOLIO I mean he'll answer the challenge,

dares, being dared.

MERCUTIO Alas, poor Romeo, he is already dead: stabbed with
a white wench's black eye; run through the ear with a love-
song; the very pin of his heart cleft with the blind bow-boy's   15
butt-shaft. And is he a man to encounter Tybalt?

BENVOLIO Why, what is Tybalt?

MERCUTIO More than Prince of Cats. O he's the courageous
captain of compliments. He fights as you sing prick-song;
keeps time, distance, and proportion; he rests his minim rests,   20
one, two, and the third in your bosom; the very butcher of a
silk button, a duellist, a duellist; a gentleman of the very first
house, of the first and second cause. Ah, the immortal
passado! The *punto reverso!* The *hay!*

BENVOLIO The what?   25

MERCUTIO The pox of such antic, lisping, affecting fantasticoes;
these new tuners of accent! "By Jesu, a very good blade!
A very tall man! A very good whore!" Why, is not this a
lamentable thing, grandsire, that we should be thus afflicted
with these strange flies, these fashion-mongers, these "pardon   30
me's" who stand so much on the new form that they cannot sit
at ease on the old bench? O, their bones, their bones!

Enter ROMEO

BENVOLIO Here comes Romeo, here comes Romeo.

MERCUTIO Without his roe, like a dried herring. O flesh, flesh,
how art thou fishified! Now is he for the numbers that   35
Petrarch flowed in. Laura, to his lady, was a kitchen-wench—
marry, she had a better love to be-rhyme her; Dido, a dowdy;
Cleopatra, a gipsy; Helen and Hero, hildings and harlots;

He'll dare to accept the dare.

MERCUTIO Oh, poor Romeo. He's as good as dead! Stabbed with a
look from Rosaline's dark eyes, shot through the ear with a
love-song. The center of his heart pierced by an arrow from   15
Cupid. And is such a man a match for Tybalt?

BENVOLIO Why, who is Tybalt?

MERCUTIO More than the Prince of Cats from the old fable, I can
tell you. Oh, he's very good at dueling. He fights as
you read music—keeping good time and rhythm. He pauses   20
one, two, then on three he stabs you. He can butcher any shirt
button he chooses. He's the best duelist you can find.
He has such quick moves—the *passado,* the *punto reverse*—and then
performs the triumphant *Hey*!

BENVOLIO The what?   25

MERCUTIO Oh, a plague on all these weird, lisping, attitude-posing,
affected fops, these freaks of fashion. "By God, a very good blade!
A very tall man! A very good whore!" Isn't it disgusting, old
man, that we should have to put up with all these parasites, these
fashion followers, these "pardon me's," who stand so much on   30
proper form they can't sit without a formal prop. Oh, their "bon"
this and their "bon" that.

Enter ROMEO

BENVOLIO Here comes Romeo! Here comes Romeo!

MERCUTIO Without his Roe-saline, he's like a dried herring. Oh flesh,
flesh, how fishy you look! Now he'll be writing sonnets as   35
Petrarch did to Laura, but Laura's a kitchen maid compared to Romeo's
lady, although Laura did have a better poet writing to her; Dido will
seem dull; Cleopatra, a gypsy; Helen and Hero, sluts and harlots;

Thisbe, a grey eye or so, but not to the purpose. Signior

Romeo, *bon jour!* There's French salutation to your French　　40

slop. You gave us the counterfeit fairly last night.

ROMEO　Good morrow to you both. What counterfeit did I

give you?

MERCUTIO　The slip, sir, the slip. Can you not conceive?

ROMEO　Pardon, good Mercutio; my business was great, and　　45

in such a case as mine a man may strain courtesy.

MERCUTIO　That's as much as to say, such a case as yours

constrains a man to bow in the hams.

ROMEO　Meaning to curtsy.

MERCUTIO　Thou hast most kindly hit it.　　50

ROMEO　A most courteous exposition.

MERCUTIO　Nay, I am the very pink of courtesy.

ROMEO　Pink for flower.

MERCUTIO　Right.

ROMEO　Why, then is my pump well flowered.　＊ shoe　　55

MERCUTIO　Sure wit! Follow me this jest now, till thou hast worn out

thy pump, that when the single sole of it is worn, the jest may remain,

after the wearing, solely singular.

ROMEO　O single-soled jest, solely singular for the singleness!

MERCUTIO　Come between us, good Benvolio; my wits faint.　　60

ROMEO　Switch and spurs, switch and spurs; or I'll cry a match.

MERCUTIO　Nay, if our wits run the wild-goose chase, I am

done. For thou hast more of the wild goose in one of thy wits

than, I am sure, I have in my whole five. Was I with you there

for the goose?　　65

ROMEO　Thou wast never with me for anything when thou

Thisbe, even though she had grey eyes, can't compete.

Well, Romeo, *bonjour*—that's French to match your French   40

style pants. You played a trick on us last night.

ROMEO Good morning to you both. What trick did

    I play?

MERCUTIO The slip. You gave us the slip—get it?

ROMEO I'm sorry, Mercutio, but my business was important, and in   45

    such a case, a man may bend the rules of courtesy.

MERCUTIO That's like saying you had to bow out.

    Is that it?

ROMEO Meaning to curtsy?

MERCUTIO You've got it.   50

ROMEO A most courteous explanation.

MERCUTIO Oh, yes, I'm the very flower of courtesy.

ROMEO A flower, hmmm? The pink?

MERCUTIO Right.

ROMEO In that case, my pinked shoe is well flowered.   55

MERCUTIO Clever. But the joke is wearing thin, as will

    your shoe, and nothing will be left but the

    sole of the joke.

ROMEO A single sole joke, singular solely for its silliness.

MERCUTIO Part us, good Benvolio, I'm at my wits' end.   60

ROMEO Use a whip and spurs on it to keep going or I win!

MERCUTIO Well, if our wits are off on a wild goose chase,

    I give up, for you have more of the wild goose in one

    of your wits than I have in all five. Am I even with you

    now in this goose business?   65

ROMEO You were never with me anywhere when you

wast not there for the goose.

MERCUTIO I will bite thee by the ear for that jest.

ROMEO Nay, good goose, bite not.

MERCUTIO Thy wit is a very bitter sweeting; it is most sharp   70
sauce.

ROMEO And is it not then well served in to a sweet goose?

MERCUTIO O, here's a wit of cheveril, that stretches from an
inch narrow to an ell broad!

ROMEO I stretch it out for that word "broad," which, added to   75
the goose, proves thee far and wide a broad goose.

MERCUTIO Why, is not this better now than groaning for love?
Now art thou sociable, now art thou Romeo; now art thou
what thou art by art as well as by nature; for this drivelling
love is like a great natural that runs lolling up and down to   80
hide his bauble in a hole.

BENVOLIO Stop there, stop there.

MERCUTIO Thou desirest me to stop in my tale against the hair.

BENVOLIO Thou wouldst else have made thy tale large.

MERCUTIO O, thou art deceived: I would have made it short;   85
for I was come to the whole depth of my tale, and meant,
indeed, to occupy the argument no longer.

ROMEO Here's goodly gear!

Enter NURSE *and her man,* PETER

A sail, a sail!

BENVOLIO Two, two; a shirt and a smock.   90

NURSE Peter!

PETER Anon.

NURSE My fan, Peter.

weren't there for the goose.

MERCUTIO I'll bite your ear for that.

ROMEO Be a good goose and don't bite.

MERCUTIO Your wit just bit—bittersweetly. It is a most   70
sharp sauce.

ROMEO Then it's perfect to fill a sweet goose with.

MERCUTIO Oh, here's an elastic wit
that stretches from an inch to a yard.

ROMEO I stretched it wide for that word "big," because you're   75
known far and wide as a big goose.

MERCUTIO Now, isn't this more fun than groaning for love?
Now you're sociable, now you're more yourself. Now
you're what you are by art as well as by nature. This
drooling love is like some idiot who runs around trying   80
to hide his worthless treasure.

BENVOLIO Stop there, stop right there.

MERCUTIO You want me to stop before the punchline?

BENVOLIO Otherwise, you'd go on forever.

MERCUTIO No, you're quite wrong. I would have made it short,   85
I was almost finished and meant, indeed, to keep up the
matter in question no longer.

ROMEO Look at that; it's quite an outfit,

Enter NURSE *and her servant* PETER

I see a sail!

BENVOLIO No, two! Two! His and hers.   90

NURSE Peter!

PETER Right away!

NURSE Give me my fan, Peter.

MERCUTIO Good Peter, to hide her face; for her fan's the
    fairer face.   95

NURSE God ye good morrow, gentlemen.

MERCUTIO God ye good den, fair gentlewoman.

NURSE Is it good den?

MERCUTIO 'Tis no less, I tell ye; for the bawdy hand of the dial *Tease each other*
    is now upon the prick of noon.   100

NURSE Out upon you! What a man are you?

ROMEO One, gentlewoman, that God hath made for himself
    to mar.

NURSE By my troth, it is well said. "For himself to mar" quoth 'a.
    Gentlemen, can any of you tell me where I may find the   105
    young Romeo?

ROMEO I can tell you; but young Romeo will be older when
    you have found him than he was when you sought him. I am
    the youngest of that name, for fault of a worse.

NURSE You say well.   110

MERCUTIO Yea, is the worst well? Very well too, i' faith;
    wisely, wisely.

NURSE If you be he, sir, I desire some confidence with you.

BENVOLIO She will indite him to some supper.

MERCUTIO A bawd, a bawd, a bawd! So, Ho!   115

ROMEO What hast thou found?

MERCUTIO No hare, sir; unless a hare, sir, in a Lenten pie, that
    is something stale and hoar ere it be spent. [*He sings*]
        An old hare hoar,
        And an old hare hoar,   120
        Is very good meat in Lent;

MERCUTIO Yes, Peter, to hide her face.

    The fan is prettier. 95

NURSE Good morning, gentlemen.

MERCUTIO Good afternoon, fair gentlewoman.

NURSE Is it afternoon?

MERCUTIO It must be, for the horny hand of the clock

    stands erect at twelve. 100

NURSE Shame on you! What sort of man are you?

ROMEO Gentlewoman, he's one that God made, but he

    mars himself.

NURSE My word, that's well said: "He mars himself,"

    he said. Gentlemen, can any of you tell me where 105

    I may find the young Romeo?

ROMEO I can tell you, but young Romeo will be older when

    you find him than when you went looking for him. I

    am the youngest of that name, for lack of a worse one.

NURSE You put things well. 110

MERCUTIO Oh, so "worse" is well put?

    How clever of you. How wise.

NURSE If you're Romeo, I'd like to talk to you in confidence.

BENVOLIO She will "indite" him to have supper.

MERCUTIO A pimp! A pimp! A pimp! Tally ho! 115

ROMEO What have you found?

MERCUTIO Not a rabbit, unless it's a hare in a pie for Lent,

    somewhat mouldy and stale before it gets eaten. [*He sings*]

        A mouldy old hare

        And a hairy old whore 120

        Are very good meat in Lent.

But a hare that is hoar

Is too much for a score,

When it hoars ere it be spent.

Romeo, will you come to your father's? We'll to   125
dinner thither.

ROMEO   I will follow you.

MERCUTIO   Farewell ancient lady. Farewell, [*Sings*] "Lady, lady, lady."

                                 Exeunt MERCUTIO *and* BENVOLIO

NURSE   I pray you, sir, what saucy merchant was this that was
so full of his ropery?   130

ROMEO   A gentleman, nurse, that loves to hear himself talk,
and will speak more in a minute than he will stand to in a
month.

NURSE   An 'a speak anything against me, I'll take him down,
an 'a were lustier than he is and twenty such Jacks; and if I   135
cannot, I'll find those that shall. Scurvy knave! I am none of his
flirt-gills; I am none of his skain's-mates. [*To Peter*] And thou must
stand by too, and suffer every knave to use me at his pleasure?

PETER   I saw no man use you at his pleasure. If I had, my
weapon should quickly have been out, I warrant you. I dare   140
draw as soon as another man, if I see occasion in a good quarrel,
and the law is on my side.

NURSE   Now, afore God, I am so vexed that every part about
me quivers. Scurvy knave! Pray you sir, a word: and as I told
you, my young lady bid me inquire you out. What she bid me   145
say I will keep to myself. But first let me tell ye, if ye should
lead her in a fool's paradise, as they say, it were a very gross
kind of behavior, as they say; for the gentlewoman is young,

But a mouldy old whore

Can never hope to score;

For money on mould's not money well spent.

Romeo, let's go to your father's house.   125

We can have dinner there together.

ROMEO I'll follow in a moment.

MERCUTIO Farewell, ancient lady, farewell. [*Sings*] "Lady, lady, lady"

Exit MERCUTIO *and* BENVOLIO

NURSE Well, that's some farewell. Tell me, who was that,

so pleased with his own vulgarity?   130

ROMEO A gentleman, Nurse, who loves to hear himself talk.

He'll say more in a minute than he'll listen to in a

month.

NURSE If he says anything against me, I'll make a charge—even if

he were bigger and there were twenty such as him. And if I   135

cannot, I'll find someone who can. Rotten rat! I'm not one

of his silly flirts. I'm not one of his sluts! [*To Peter*] And

you just stood there and let him use me at his pleasure.

PETER I saw no man use you for his pleasure. If I had, I'd

have drawn my sword, I assure you. I dare draw it as   140

soon as any man, if I see a chance in a quarrel, and the

law is on my side.

NURSE Now, I swear, I'm so upset that every part of me

quivers. What a rotten rascal! Now, sir, I'd like a word

with you. As I said, my mistress sent me to find you.   145

What else she said, I'll keep to myself. But first, let me

tell you that if you should lead her into a fool's paradise,

as they say, that would be very wrong of you, as they say.

and therefore, if you should deal double with her, truly it
were an ill thing to be offered to any gentlewoman, and very   150
weak dealing. *wants to make sure his intensions are good.*

ROMEO Nurse, commend me to thy lady and mistress. I
protest unto thee—

NURSE Good heart, and i' faith, I will tell her as much.
Lord, Lord! She will be a joyful woman.   155

ROMEO What wilt thou tell her, nurse? Thou dost not
mark me.

NURSE I will tell her, sir, that you do protest. Which, as I take
it, is a gentlemanlike offer.

ROMEO Bid her devise   160
Some means to come to shrift this afternoon,
And there she shall at Friar Lawrence' cell
Be shrived and married. Here is for thy pains.

NURSE No, truly, sir; not a penny.

ROMEO Go to—I say you shall.   165

NURSE This afternoon, sir? Well, she shall be there.

ROMEO And stay, good Nurse behind the abbey wall,
Within this hour my man shall be with thee,
And bring thee cords made like a tackled stair,
Which to the high top-gallant of my joy   170
Must be my convoy in the secret night.
Farewell, be trusty, and I'll quit thy pains.
Farewell, commend me to thy mistress.

NURSE Now God in heaven bless thee! Hark you sir.

ROMEO What sayest thou, my dear Nurse?   175

NURSE Is your man secret? Did you ne'er hear say

She is very young. And if you try to deceive her, truly,

it would be very wicked to do to any gentlewoman, and a   150

very fickle act.

ROMEO Nurse, remember me to your lady and mistress.

I protest to you—

NURSE Good heart, I promise to tell her that.

My, my, she will be a joyful woman.   155

ROMEO What will you tell her, Nurse?

You didn't let me finish.

NURSE I will tell her, sir, that you protest, which, as I take it,

is a gentlemanly proposal.

ROMEO Tell her to plan   160

Some way to go to confession this afternoon,

And there at Friar Lawrence's cell

She'll find absolution and a husband. This is for your trouble.

NURSE No, sir, I couldn't take a penny.

ROMEO Come on, take it.   165

NURSE You said this afternoon? Well, she shall be there.

ROMEO Now wait behind the abbey wall, dear Nurse.

And my man will be there within an hour.

He'll bring you a rope ladder such as sailors use,

Which to the highest mast of my joy,   170

Will serve as my path in the dark of night.

Farewell, be loyal, and I'll reward you.

Farewell, give my love to your mistress.

NURSE May God in heaven bless you. Listen sir.

ROMEO What is it, dear Nurse?   175

NURSE Can your man keep a secret? Haven't you heard

Two may keep counsel, putting one away?

ROMEO I warrant thee my man's as true as steel.

NURSE Well, sir. My mistress is the sweetest lady. Lord, lord!
when 'twas a little prating thing! O, there is a nobleman   180
in town, one Paris, that would fain lay knife aboard. But she,
good soul, had as lief see a toad, a very toad, as see him. I
anger her sometimes, and tell her that Paris is the properer
man. But, I'll warrant you, when I say so, she looks as pale as
any clout in the versal world. Doth not rosemary and Romeo   185
begin both with a letter.

ROMEO Ay, Nurse. What of that? Both with an R.

NURSE Ah, mocker! That's the dog's name. R is for the—no,
I know it begins with some other letter. And she hath the
prettiest sententious of it, of you and rosemary, that it would   190
do you good to hear it.

ROMEO Commend me to thy lady.

NURSE Ay, a thousand times. Peter!

PETER Anon.

NURSE Before and apace.   195

Exeunt

Scene 5 *[Capulet's orchard]*

Enter JULIET

JULIET The clock struck nine when I did send the Nurse;
In half an hour she promised to return.
Perchance she cannot meet him. That's not so.

Two may keep a secret, if one of them is dead.

ROMEO I assure you, my man is true as steel.

NURSE Well, sir, my mistress is the sweetest lady. Lord, lord!
    Why when she was just a babbling child—Oh— 180
    There is a nobleman in town, named Paris,
    who would like to have her for himself, but she,
    good soul, would just as soon see a toad, a real toad, as
    see him. I tease her and tell her that Paris is the better
    man for her, but when I say that she turns pale as a sheet. 185
    Don't rosemary and Romeo begin with the same letter?

ROMEO Yes, Nurse, what about it? Both start with "R."

NURSE Don't make fun of me! "R" is what a dog says. No, I
    know it begins with some other letter, and she has the
    prettiest sayings about it, of you and rosemary. You 190
    would enjoy hearing them.

ROMEO Remember me to your lady.

NURSE Yes, a thousand times. Peter!

PETER Right away!

NURSE Go in front of me and be quick about it. 195

                   Exit

Scene 5 [*Capulet's orchard*]

Enter JULIET

JULIET The clock struck nine when I sent the Nurse.
    She promised to return in half an hour.
    Maybe she couldn't find him. That couldn't be.

O, she is lame! Love's heralds should be thoughts,
Which ten times faster glide than the sun's beams,   5
Driving back shadows over louring hills.
Therefore do nimble-pinioned doves draw Love,
And therefore hath the wind-swift Cupid wings.
Now is the sun upon the highmost hill
Of this day's journey; and from nine till twelve   10
Is three long hours, and yet she is not come.
Had she affections and warm youthful blood,
She would be as swift in motion as a ball.
My words would bandy her to my sweet love,
And his to me.   15
But old folks, many feign as they were dead,
Unwieldy, slow, heavy, and pale as lead.

              Enter NURSE *and* PETER

O God, she comes! O, honey nurse, what news?
Hast thou met with him? Send thy man away.

NURSE Peter, stay at the gate.   20

                          PETER *exits*

JULIET Now, good sweet nurse—O Lord, why look'st thou sad?
Though news be sad, yet tell them merrily.
If good, thou shamest the music of sweet news
By playing it to me with so sour a face.

NURSE I am aweary! Give me leave awhile.   25
Fie, how my bones ache! What a jaunce have I!

JULIET I would thou hadst my bones, and I thy news.
Nay, come, I pray thee, speak; good, good Nurse, speak.

NURSE Jesu, what haste? Can you not stay awhile?

She drags her feet. Love's messengers, like thoughts,
Should glide ten times faster than sunbeams,   5
Driving back shadows from darkened hills.
That's why fast-winged doves draw Venus' chariot
And that's why Cupid's wings are swift as wind.
Now the sun has arrived overhead
In this day's journey, and from nine to noon   10
Has been three long hours, yet she's not here.
If she had feelings and warm youthful blood,
She would be as swift in motion as a ball.
My words would hurl her to my sweet love,
And his would hurl her back to me.   15
But old folks act as if they're almost dead,
Unwieldy, slow, heavy, and dull as lead.

Enter NURSE *and* PETER

Thank God, she comes! Oh, dear Nurse, what news?
Have you met with him? Send Peter away.
NURSE Peter, wait at the gate.   20

PETER *exits*

JULIET Now, good, sweet Nurse—Lord, why do you look so sad?
    Even if it's sad news, tell it merrily.
    If it's good news, you spoil the music
    By playing it to me with such a sour face.
NURSE I'm tired. Let me rest a minute.   25
    My bones ache. What a rough journey I've had.
JULIET I wish you had my bones and I your news.
    Come, please tell me. Good Nurse, speak.
NURSE Lord, what haste! Can't you wait a minute?

Do you not see that I am out of breath?   30

JULIET How art thou out of breath, when thou hast breath

To say to me that thou art out of breath?

The excuse that thou dost make in this delay

Is longer than the tale thou dost excuse.

Is thy news good or bad? Answer to that.   35

Say either, and I'll stay the circumstance.

Let me be satisfied, is't good or bad?

NURSE Well, you have made a simple choice! You know not

how to choose a man. Romeo? No, not he. Though his face be

better than any man's, yet his leg excels all men's. And for a   40

hand, and a foot, and a body, though they be not to be talked

on, yet they are past compare. He is not the flower of

courtesy, but I'll warrant him as gentle as a lamb. Go thy

ways, wench, serve God. What, have you dined at home?

JULIET No, no. But all this did I know before.   45

What says he of our marriage? What of that?

NURSE Lord, how my head aches! What a head have I!

It beats as it would fall in twenty pieces.

My back o' t'other side! Ah, my back, my back!

Beshew your heart for sending me about   50

To catch my death with jaunting up and down!

JULIET I' faith, I am sorry that thou art not well.

Sweet, sweet, sweet nurse, tell me, what says my love?

NURSE Your love says, like an honest gentleman, and a

courteous, and a kind, and a handsome, and I warrant, a   55

virtuous—Where is your Mother?

JULIET Where is my mother! Why, she is within.

Can't you see I am out of breath?   30

JULIET How can you be out of breath when you have breath

To tell me that you're out of breath?

The excuse you make takes you

Much longer than the news you bring.

Is your news good or bad? Tell me that.   35

Say either, and I'll do without the details.

Just tell me: is it good or bad?

NURSE Well, you've made a foolish choice. You don't know how to

choose a man. Romeo? No, not him. Although his face is better

than any man's. And his legs excel any others'. And his hands   40

and feet and body, although there's nothing to say about them,

still, they are past compare. He is not the flower of courtesy, but I

found him gentle as a lamb. Well, off you go, girl, as God has willed.

Now then, have you dined at home?

JULIET No, no. But all of this I knew before.   45

What does he say about our wedding? What about that?

NURSE Lord, how my head aches. What a headache I have!

It pounds as if it's going to break in twenty pieces.

My back, too. On the other side. Ah, my back, my back.

Shame on you for sending me out,   50

To catch my death with chasing all about.

JULIET I'm truly sorry that you are not well.

Sweet, sweet, sweet Nurse, tell me, what does my love say?

NURSE Your love says, like an honest gentleman and a

courteous, and a kind, and a handsome, and, I'll bet,   55

a virtuous—where is your mother?

JULIET Where is my mother? Why, she's inside.

Where should she be? How oddly thou repliest!
"Your love says like an honest gentleman,
'Where is your mother?'" 60
NURSE O God's lady dear!
Are you so hot? Marry, come up, I trow.
Is this the poultice for my aching bones?
Henceforward, do your messages yourself.
JULIET Here's such a coil! Come, what says Romeo? 65
NURSE Have you got leave to go to shrift today?
JULIET I have.
NURSE Then hie you hence to Friar Lawrence' cell.
There stays a husband to make you a wife.
Now comes the wanton blood up in your cheeks. 70
They'll be in scarlet straight at any news.
Hie you to church. I must another way
To fetch a ladder, by the which your love
Must climb a bird's nest soon, when it is dark.
I am the drudge, and toil in your delight, 75
But you shall bear the burden soon at night.
Go. I'll to dinner. Hie you to the cell!
JULIET Hie to high fortune! Honest Nurse, farewell!

Exeunt

Scene 6 [*Friar Lawrence's cell*]

Enter FRIAR LAWRENCE *and* ROMEO
FRIAR LAWRENCE   So smile the heaven upon this holy act
That after-hours with sorrow chide us not!
ROMEO Amen, amen! But come what sorrow can,

Where else would she be? What an odd answer:

"Your love says, like an honest gentleman,

'Where is your mother?'"   60

NURSE Oh, Blessed Mary,

Are you so eager? Well, I'll be.

Is this relief to soothe my aching bones?

From now on, run your own messages.

JULIET What a fuss! Come on, what did Romeo say?   65

NURSE Have you got permission to go to confession today?

JULIET Yes, I have.

NURSE Then go right away to Friar Lawrence.

There waits a husband to make you a wife.

Now the blood has rushed to your cheeks;   70

Any more news, and you'll turn scarlet.

Get to church. I'm going somewhere

To fetch a ladder by which your love

May climb to your room, when it grows dark.

I am the drudge who toils for your delight, "while you're   75
getting married

But you'll be the one working hard tonight. I'm working to set up!"

Go. I'm off to dine. Go to the priest's cell.

JULIET I'm off to good fortune, honest Nurse, farewell.

                                                                    Exit

Scene 6 [*Friar Lawrence's cell.*]

                        Enter FRIAR LAWRENCE *and* ROMEO

FRIAR LAWRENCE May the heavens so bless this holy act hopes to
bring families
That later times won't punish us with sorrow. together w/ this
marriage
ROMEO Amen to that. But if sorrow does come

107

It cannot countervail the exchange of joy

That one short minute gives me in her sight.   5

Do thou but close our hands with holy words,

Then love-devouring death do what he dare.

It is enough I may but call her mine.

FRIAR LAWRENCE   These violent delights have violent ends, > on TEST!

And in their triumph die; like fire and powder,   10

Which, as they kiss, consume. The sweetest honey

Is loathsome in his own deliciousness,

And in the taste confounds the appetite.

Therefore love moderately; long love doth so.

Too swift arrives as tardy as too slow. > take it easy   15

Enter JULIET

Here comes the lady. O, so light a foot

Will ne'er wear out the everlasting flint.

A lover may bestride the gossamers

That idles in the wanton summer air,

And yet not fall, so light is vanity.   20

JULIET   Good even to my ghostly confessor.

FRIAR LAWRENCE   Romeo shall thank thee, daughter, for us both.

JULIET   As much to him, else is his thanks too much.

ROMEO   Ah, Juliet, if the measure of thy joy

Be heaped like mine, and that thy skill be more   25

To blazon it, then sweeten with thy breath

This neighbor air, and let rich music's tongue

Unfold the imagined happiness that both

Receive in either by this dear encounter.

JULIET   Conceit, more rich in matter than in words,   30

It cannot outweigh the exchange of joy

That one short minute in her sight gives to me.   5

If you just join our hands with holy words,

Then love-devouring death can try his worst.

It's enough that I may call her mine.

FRIAR LAWRENCE These violent emotions have violent ends,

And at their peak they die, like fire and gun powder,   10

Which, when they meet, consume each other. The sweetest honey

Is sickening in excess,   > foreshadowing

And eating it spoils the appetite.

So love moderately, if you want it to last.

In a long race the slow get there as soon as the fast.   15

Enter JULIET

Here comes the lady. Oh, such a light step

Will never wear down this road.

A lover can walk on spider threads

That float in the playful summer breeze

And yet not fall, so light is earthly love.   20

JULIET Good evening to my spiritual father.

FRIAR LAWRENCE Romeo will kiss you, daughter, for us both.

JULIET And to be fair, I'll return his kiss.

ROMEO Oh, Juliet, if the fullness of your joy's

As great as mine, and since you're better at   25

Describing it, then with your words perfume

The air around us; let rich music's voice

Unfold the imagined happiness that we both

Of us share in this meeting here.

JULIET Thoughts more rich in meaning than mere words   30

Brags of his substance, not of ornament.

They are but beggars that can count their worth;

But my true love is grown to such excess

I cannot sum up half my sum of wealth.

FRIAR LAWRENCE Come, come with me, and we will   35
    make short work.

For, by your leaves, you shall not stay alone   > marries

Till holy church incorporate two in one.   them

Exeunt

Proudly boast of substance, not ornamental phrases.

Those who can count their worth are beggars;

But my true love has grown so much

I cannot sum up half my sum of wealth.

FRIAR LAWRENCE Come, come along with me, and we   35

      will soon have the deed done,

For, I think, you should not stay alone

Till holy church has made you one.

They exit

With Shakespeare, weather is very important!

Act Three

Scene 1 [*A street in Verona*]

Enter MERCUTIO, BENVOLIO, *and* MEN

BENVOLIO I pray thee, good Mercutio, let's retire;

The day is hot, the Capels are abroad,

And if we meet, we shall not 'scape a brawl,

For now, these hot days, is the mad blood stirring.

MERCUTIO Thou art like one of these fellows that, when he   5

enters the confines of a tavern, clasps me his sword upon the

table and says, "God send me no need of thee"; and by the

operation of the second cup, draws him on the drawer, when

indeed there is no need.

BENVOLIO Am I like such a fellow?   10

MERCUTIO Come, come, thou art as hot a Jack in thy mood as

any in Italy; and as soon moved to be moody, and as soon

moody to be moved.

BENVOLIO And what to?

MERCUTIO Nay, an there were two such, we should have none shortly,   15

for one would kill the other. Thou? Why, thou wilt quarrel with

a man that hath a hair more or a hair less in his beard than thou

hast. Thou wilt quarrel with a man for cracking nuts, having no

other reason but because thou hast hazel eyes. What eye but

such an eye would spy out such a quarrel? Thy head is as full   20

of quarrels as an egg is full of meat, and yet thy head

hath been beaten as addle as an egg for quarreling. Thou hast

quarreled with a man for coughing in the street, because he

hath wakened thy dog that hath lain asleep in the sun.

Act Three

Scene 1 [*A street in Verona*]

Enter MERCUTIO, BENVOLIO, *and* MEN

BENVOLIO   Come on, Mercutio, let's go back.

It's hot, and the Capulets are out on the town.

If we meet, we won't escape a brawl,

For these hot days stir up the blood.

MERCUTIO You're like one of those fellows who enters a tavern and   5

slaps his sword on the table and says, "God send me no need

of this!" and then by the second drink, you're drawing your

sword on the waiter who served you the drinks, when

he hasn't done anything to you.

> saying he would fight / argue about anything

BENVOLIO   Am I really like that?   10

MERCUTIO   Come on, you're as hot tempered a man as any

in Italy, as soon made moody and as soon

in a mood to be made angry.

BENVOLIO   And what to?

MERCUTIO   To? Why if there were two of you, there'd soon be none,   15

for one would kill the other. Why you'd even quarrel

with a man for having one hair more or less in his beard

than you have. You'd quarrel with a man who was cracking nuts

for no more reason than that you have hazel eyes. Who else

but you would see an offense in that? Your head is as full   20

of quarrels as an egg is full of meat. And yet you've had

your head beaten as an egg is scrambled, for quarreling.

You've quarreled with a man for coughing in the street

because he woke up your dog that was sleeping in the sun.

> again saying he argues about everything

113

Didst thou not fall out with a tailor for wearing   25

his new doublet before Easter? With another,

for tying his new shoes with old riband? And yet thou

wilt tutor me from quarreling!

BENVOLIO And I were so apt to quarrel as thou art, any man

should buy the fee simple of my life for an hour and a quarter.   30

MERCUTIO The fee simple! O simple!

Enter TYBALT, PETRUCHIO, *and others*

BENVOLIO By my head, here come the Capulets.

MERCUTIO By my heel, I care not.

TYBALT Follow me close, for I will speak to them.

Gentlemen, good den; a word with one of you.   35

MERCUTIO And but one word with one of us? Couple it with

something. Make it a word and a blow.

TYBALT You shall find me apt enough to that, sir, an you will

give me occasion.

MERCUTIO Could you not take some occasion without giving?   40

TYBALT Mercutio, thou consortest with Romeo.

MERCUTIO Consort? What, dost thou make us minstrels? An

thou make minstrels of us, look to hear nothing but discords.

Here's my fiddlestick, here's that shall make you dance.

Zounds, consort!   45

BENVOLIO We talk here in the public haunt of men.

Either withdraw unto some private place,

And reason coldly of your grievances,

Or else depart. Here all eyes gaze on us.

Didn't you quarrel with a tailor for wearing his new jacket   25

before Easter, and with another man for tying his new shoes

with old laces? And you're going to teach me how to stay

out of a fight?

BENVOLIO If I were apt to quarrel as much as you say, whoever bought

my life would own it for only an hour and a quarter.   30

MERCUTIO Bought your life? What a poor joke!

Enter TYBALT, PETRUCHIO, *and others*

BENVOLIO By my head, here come the Capulets.

MERCUTIO By my heel, I don't care.

TYBALT Follow me close, for I will speak to them.

Good afternoon, gentlemen. I'd like a word with one of you.   35

MERCUTIO Just one word for the two of us? Add something

to that. Make it a word and a blow.

TYBALT You'll find I'm ready for that, sir, if you give

me the reason.

MERCUTIO Couldn't you find a reason without my giving you one?   40

TYBALT Mercutio, you're often in Romeo's group—

MERCUTIO His "group"? What do you think we are, a bunch of

fiddlers? If you make fiddlers of us, expect to hear nothing but

sour notes. Here's my fiddle bow, that'll make you

dance. Honestly! Group!   45

BENVOLIO We're talking out in public.

Either go with us to some private place,

Or argue quietly of your differences,

Or go your separate ways. Everyone's looking at us.

MERCUTIO Men's eyes were made to look, and let them gaze.   50
    I will not budge for no man's pleasure, I.

Enter ROMEO

TYBALT Well, peace be with you, sir, here comes my man.
MERCUTIO But I'll be hanged, sir, if he wear your livery.
    Marry, go before to field, he'll be your follower.
    Your worship in that sense may call him man.   55
TYBALT Romeo, the love I bear thee can afford
    No better term than this: thou art a villain.
ROMEO Tybalt, the reason that I have to love thee
    Doth much excuse the appertaining rage
    To such a greeting: villain am I none,   60
    Therefore farewell. I see thou knowest me not.
TYBALT Boy, this shall not excuse the injuries
    That thou hast done me, therefore turn and draw.
ROMEO I do protest I never injured thee,
    But love thee better than thou canst devise,   65
    Till thou shalt know the reason of my love.
    And so, good Capulet, which name I tender
    As dearly as mine own, be satisfied.
MERCUTIO O calm, dishonorable, vile submission:
    [*He draws*] *Alla stoccata* carries it away!   70
    Tybalt, you rat-catcher, will you walk?
TYBALT What wouldst thou have with me?
MERCUTIO Good King of Cats, nothing but one of your nine
    lives that I mean to make bold withal, and as you shall use me
    hereafter, dry-beat the rest of the eight. Will you pluck your   75
    sword out of his pilcher by the ears? Make haste, lest mine be

MERCUTIO Men's eyes were made to look, so let them gaze.   50

I'm not moving to please anyone, not I.

Enter ROMEO

TYBALT Well, peace be with you, sir, here comes my man.

MERCUTIO But I'll be hanged, sir, if he's a man of yours.

Oh, yes, if you want a fight, he'll follow you to the place.

Your highness, in that sense, may call him your man.   55

TYBALT Romeo, the best I can say of you is that you are

a villain.

ROMEO Tybalt, I have reasons to be friendly to you,

So I'll control the anger that your greeting

Has caused in me. I am no villain.   60

So, goodbye. I realize you don't really know me.

TYBALT Boy, that's no excuse for the insults you've paid me.

Turn and draw your sword.

ROMEO I here declare I never insulted you!

But hold you more a friend than you can know,   65

Until you understand why that is.

And so, dear Capulet, which name I hold

As dearly as my own, be calm.

MERCUTIO Oh, calm, dishonorable, vile submission:

[*He draws*] *Now the thrust* succeeds!   70

Tybalt, you rat catcher, will you dance with me?

TYBALT What do you want with me?

MERCUTIO Good King of Cats, nothing but one of your nine

lives. I mean to have it, and I'll beat up on the other eight if

you continue to insult us. Will you draw your sword from its   75

scabbard by its ears? Hurry up, or mine will be about your

[Handwritten margin notes: "he can't mistreat him because they're now related" and a quotation mark near line 65]

117

about your ears ere it be out.

TYBALT I am for you. [*He draws*]

ROMEO Gentle Mercutio, put thy rapier up.

MERCUTIO Come sir, your *passado*. [*They fight*] 80

ROMEO Draw, Benvolio, beat down their weapons.

Gentlemen, for shame, forbear this outrage.

Tybalt! Mercutio! The Prince expressly hath

Forbid this bandying in Verona streets.

Hold, Tybalt! Good Mercutio! 85

TYBALT *under* ROMEO's *arm wounds* MERCUTIO

PETRUCHIO Away, Tybalt!

Exit TYBALT *with his followers*

MERCUTIO I am hurt.

A plague o' both houses. I am sped.

Is he gone, and hath nothing?

BENVOLIO What, art thou hurt? 90

MERCUTIO Ay, ay, a scratch, a scratch. Marry, 'tis enough.

Where's my page? Go villain, fetch a surgeon.

Exit PAGE

ROMEO Courage man, the hurt cannot be much.

MERCUTIO No 'tis not so deep as a well, not so wide as a church

door, but 'tis enough, 'twill serve. Ask for me tomorrow and 95

you shall find me a grave man. I am peppered, I warrant, for >dying &

this world. A plague o' both your houses. Zounds, a dog, a making

puns

rat, a mouse, a cat, to scratch a man to death. A braggart, a

rogue, a villain, that fights by the book of arithmetic—why the

devil came you between us? I was hurt under your arm. 100

ROMEO I thought all for the best.

MERCUTIO Help me into some house, Benvolio,

ears before yours is out.

TYBALT   I am at your service. [He *draws*]

ROMEO   Dear Mercutio, put your sword away.

MERCUTIO   Come on, show me your best thrust. [*They fight*]   80

ROMEO   Draw your sword, Benvolio. Beat down their weapons.

Shame on you gentlemen. Stop this fighting.

Tybalt! Mercutio! You know the Prince has

Forbidden fighting in the streets of Verona.

Stop, Tybalt! Please, Mercutio!   85

TYBALT *stabs* MERCUTIO *under* ROMEO'S *arm*

PETRUCHIO   Flee, Tybalt!

Exit TYBALT *and his men*

MERCUTIO   I am hurt.

A curse on both families. I'm finished.

Has he gone? Gotten away without a wound?

BENVOLIO   What! Are you hurt?   90

MERCUTIO   Yes, yes, a scratch, a scratch, but it's enough.

Where's my servant? Go, you rascal, get me a doctor.

Exit PAGE

ROMEO   Courage man, the wound cannot be much.

MERCUTIO   No, it's not as deep as a well, nor as wide as a church
   door, but it's enough. It will do. Ask for me tomorrow, and   95
   you'll find me a grave man. I am finished, I assure you, for
   this world. A curse on both your families. Damn—that a dog,
   a rat, a mouse, a cat could scratch a man to death. A braggart
   a rogue, a villain, that fights by a textbook. Why the devil
   did you get between us? I was stabbed under your arm!   100

ROMEO   I was trying to stop the fight.

MERCUTIO   Help me into some nearby house, Benvolio,

Or I shall faint. A plague o' both your houses,

They have made worms' meat of me.

I have it, and soundly too. Your houses! 105

Exit MERCUTIO *and* BENVOLIO

ROMEO This gentleman, the Prince's near ally,

My very friend, hath got this mortal hurt

In my behalf—my reputation stained

With Tybalt's slander—Tybalt that an hour

Hath been my cousin. O sweet Juliet, 110

Thy beauty hath made me effeminate

And in my temper softened valor's steel.

Enter BENVOLIO

BENVOLIO O Romeo, Romeo, brave Mercutio is dead.

That gallant spirit hath aspired the clouds

Which too untimely here did scorn the earth. 115

ROMEO This day's black fate on more days doth depend:

This but begins the woe others must end.

Enter TYBALT

BENVOLIO Here comes the furious Tybalt back again.

ROMEO Alive in triumph, and Mercutio slain.

Away to heaven respective lenity, 120

And fire-eyed fury be my conduct now!

Now Tybalt, take the "villain" back again

That late thou gav'st me, for Mercutio's soul

Is but a little way above our heads,

Staying for thine to keep him company. 125

Either thou or I, or both, must go with him.

TYBALT Thou wretched boy, that did consort him here,

Or I shall faint. A curse on both your families.

They have made worms' meat of me.

I've had it, well and truly. Your families—   105

Exit MERCUTIO *and* BENVOLIO

ROMEO This gentleman, the Prince's relative,

My own true friend, got this mortal wound

Defending my good reputation stained

By Tybalt's insult—Tybalt that for just

An hour had been my cousin. Oh, sweet Juliet,   110

Your beauty has made soft and weak

The steel-like boldness of my nature.

Enter BENVOLIO

BENVOLIO Oh, Romeo, Romeo, brave Mercutio is dead!

That gallant spirit has risen to the clouds

And much too soon has gone to heaven.   115

ROMEO This dark day's black fate will more days spend:

This just begins the woe others must end.

Enter TYBALT (Juliet's cousin)

BENVOLIO Here comes furious Tybalt back again.

ROMEO He struts in triumph while Mercutio's dead.

Well, heaven can have its mercy,   120

But fire-eyed fury is my guide now.

Now, Tybalt, take back the insults

That you spoke earlier, for Mercutio's soul

Is just up there a little way waiting

For your soul to keep him company.   125

Either you or I or both of us must join him.

TYBALT You miserable boy. You were his friend here,

Shalt with him hence.

ROMEO   This shall determine that.

They fight. TYBALT *falls*

BENVOLIO   Romeo, away, be gone!   130

    The citizens are up, and Tybalt slain!

    Stand not amazed. The Prince will doom thee death

    If thou art taken. Hence, be gone, away!

ROMEO   O, I am fortune's fool.

BENVOLIO   Why dost thou stay?   135

                                 Exit ROMEO

                    Enter CITIZENS

CITIZEN   Which way ran he that killed Mercutio?

    Tybalt, that murderer, which way ran he?

BENVOLIO   There lies that Tybalt.

CITIZEN   Up, sir, go with me.

    I charge thee in the Prince's name, obey.   140

      Enter PRINCE, MONTAGUE, CAPULET, *their* WIVES *and all*

PRINCE   Where are the vile beginners of this fray?

BENVOLIO   O noble Prince, I can discover all

    The unlucky manage of this fatal brawl.

    There lies the man, slain by young Romeo,

    That slew thy kinsman, brave Mercutio.   145

LADY CAPULET   Tybalt, my cousin, O my brother's child!

    O Prince, O husband, O the blood is spilled

    Of my dear kinsman! Prince, as thou art true,

    For blood of ours shed blood of Montague.

    O cousin, cousin!   150

PRINCE   Benvolio, who began this bloody fray?

You shall be with him there.

ROMEO Our swords will decide that.

They fight. TYBALT *falls*

BENVOLIO Romeo, away, be gone!   130

The citizens are roused, and Tybalt is dead.

Don't just stand there. The Prince will condemn you to death

If you're found here. Go, quickly!

ROMEO Oh, I am Fate's fool!

BENVOLIO Why are you standing there?   135

Exit ROMEO

Enter CITIZENS

CITIZEN Which way did Mercutio's killer go?

Tybalt, that murderer, where did he run?

BENVOLIO There lies Tybalt.

CITIZEN Get up, sir, go with me.

I charge you in the Prince's name to obey.   140

Enter PRINCE, MONTAGUE, CAPULET, *their* WIVES *and all*

PRINCE Where are the rogues who started this fight?

BENVOLIO Oh, noble Prince, I can explain it all,

The unhappy causes of this fatal brawl.

There lies the man, killed by young Romeo,

Who killed your kinsman, brave Mercutio.   145

LADY CAPULET Tybalt, my nephew, my brother's child!

Oh, Prince. Oh, husband. Oh, the blood is spilled

Of my dear kinsman! Prince, if you are just and true,

For blood of ours shed blood of Montague.

Oh, nephew, nephew.   150

PRINCE Benvolio, who started this bloody fight?

BENVOLIO Tybalt, here slain, whom Romeo's hand did slay.
    Romeo, who spoke him fair, bid him bethink
    How nice the quarrel was, and urged withal
    Your high displeasure. All this uttered   155
    With gentle breath, calm look, knees humbly bowed,
    Could not take truce with the unruly spleen
    Of Tybalt, deaf to peace, but that he tilts
    With piercing steel at bold Mercutio's breast,
    Who, all as hot, turns deadly point to point   160
    And, with a martial scorn, with one hand beats
    Cold death aside, and with the other sends
    It back to Tybalt, whose dexterity
    Retorts it. Romeo, he cries aloud
    "Hold, friends! Friends part!" and swifter than his tongue   165
    His agile arm beats down their fatal points
    And 'twixt them rushes; underneath whose arm
    An envious thrust from Tybalt hit the life
    Of stout Mercutio; and then Tybalt fled,
    But by and by comes back to Romeo,   170
    Who had but newly entertained revenge,
    And to it they go like lightning: for, ere I
    Could draw to part them, was stout Tybalt slain,
    And as he fell did Romeo turn and fly.
    This is the truth, or let Benvolio die.   175
LADY CAPULET He is a kinsman to the Montague.
    Affection makes him false. He speaks not true.
    Some twenty of them fought in this black strife
    And all those twenty could but kill one life.

BENVOLIO Tybalt, here dead, whom Romeo did slay.

    Romeo was polite to him and asked him to think

    How petty was this quarrel and reminded him

    How angry you would be. He said it   155

    All gently with a calm look, knees humbly bowed,

    But no truce could be made with the hot temper

    Of Tybalt who was deaf to peace and who aimed

    His piercing steel at bold Mercutio's chest,

    And he, just as angry, turned his sword's point,   160

    And with soldierly contempt, with one hand pushes

    Death's steel away, and with the other sends

    It back to Tybalt, who skillfully

    Repels it. Then Romeo cries out loud

    "Hold friends! Friends, part!" And faster than he spoke   165

    His agile arm knocked down their swords

    And he runs between them. Underneath his arm

    A spiteful thrust from Tybalt ends the life

    Of brave Mercutio. And then Tybalt fled,

    But by and by comes back to Romeo,   170

    Who by then had decided on revenge

    And the two of them fought like lightning. Before I

    Could separate them, brave Tybalt was killed,

    And as he fell, Romeo turned to fly.

    That is the truth, or may I die.   175

LADY CAPULET Why, he's related to that Montague.

    That makes him lie. What he says is not true.

    Some twenty of them fought in this evil strife

    And all twenty could only take one life.

I beg for justice, which thou, Prince, must give.   180
Romeo slew Tybalt. Romeo must not live.
PRINCE Romeo slew him, he slew Mercutio.
Who now the price of his dear blood doth owe?
MONTAGUE Not Romeo, Prince, he was Mercutio's friend.
His fault concludes but what the law should end,   185
The life of Tybalt.
PRINCE And for that offense
Immediately we do exile him hence.
I have an interest in your hearts' proceeding;
My blood for your rude brawls doth lie a-bleeding.   190
But I'll amerce you with so strong a fine
That you shall all repent the loss of mine.
I will be deaf to pleading and excuses.
Nor tears nor prayers shall purchase out abuses.
Therefore, use none. Let Romeo hence in haste,   195
Else, when he is found, that hour is his last.
Bear hence this body, and attend our will.
Mercy but murders, pardoning those that kill.

Exeunt

Scene 2 *[Capulet's orchard]*

Enter JULIET

JULIET Gallop apace, you fiery-footed steeds,

I beg for justice, which you, Prince, must give.   180

Romeo killed Tybalt. Romeo must not live.

PRINCE Romeo slew him, but he slew Mercutio.

Who pays the price for that death, do you know?

MONTAGUE Not Romeo, Prince, he was Mercutio's friend.

He did just what the law would do and would end   185

The life of Tybalt.

PRINCE And for that offense

Immediately do we exile him hence.

I have a personal interest in this proceeding:

My kinsman from your rude brawls lies bleeding.   190

But I'll lay on you such a heavy fine

That you'll repent this loss of mine.

I'll be deaf to pleading and excuses,

No tears, no prayers can outweigh these abuses.

Therefore don't try them. Let Romeo fly fast   195

Or else when he's found, that hour's his last.

Take away this body and wait till I make known my will.

I'll not promote more murders by pardoning those who kill.

Exit PRINCE

Scene 2 *[Capulet's orchard]*

Enter JULIET

JULIET Gallop towards evening, you horses who draw the

Towards Phoebus' lodging. Such a wagoner
As Phaeton would whip you to the west,
And bring in cloudy night immediately.
Spread thy close curtain, love-performing night,   5
That runaways' eyes may wink, and Romeo
Leap to these arms untalked of and unseen.
Lovers can see to do their amorous rites
By their own beauties; or, if love be blind,
It best agrees with night. Come, civil night,   10
Thou sober-suited matron all in black,
And learn me how to lose a winning match,
Played for a pair of stainless maidenhoods.
Hood my unmanned blood, bating in my cheeks,
With thy black mantle, till strange loves grow bold,   15
Think true love acted simple modesty.
Come night, come Romeo, come thou day in night.
For thou wilt lie upon the wings of night,
Whiter than new snow upon a raven's back.
*Come gentle night, come loving black-browed night,   20
Give me my Romeo; and when he shall die,
Take him and cut him out in little stars,
And he will make the face of heaven so fine
That all the world will be in love with night
And pay no worship to the garish sun. *   25
O I have bought the mansion of a love
But not possessed it, and though I am sold,
Not yet enjoyed. So tedious is this day
As is the night before some festival

Sun god's chariot. A driver like

His son Phaeton would whip you to the west,

And bring on darkened night immediately.

Spread your close curtain, lovers' friend, night,   5

So that hunted men may sleep,

And Romeo leap into my arms unseen.

Lovers don't need the light to see each other;

Their love illuminates them. Or, if love is blind,

It best matches the night. Come, formal night,   10

You properly dressed matron, all in black,

And teach me how to lose yet win at love

Which is played with stakes of our virginity.

Hide my wild-bird's blood, fluttering in my cheeks,

Under your black cloak till shy love grows bold,   15

And sees true love as an act of simple modesty.

Come night, come Romeo, come lighten up the night,

For you are brighter in the night

Than new snow on a raven's back.

Come gentle night, come loving, black-robed night.   20

Give me my Romeo, and when he dies,

Take him and cut him up into little stars

And he will make the face of heaven look so fine

That all the world will be in love with night

And pay no attention to the gaudy sun.   25

Oh, I have bought the mansion of a love

But not yet taken possession, and though I am sold,

The owner hasn't claimed me yet. So long is this day,

Just like the night before some festival

To an impatient child that hath new robes   30
And may not wear them. O, here comes my Nurse.

Enter NURSE *with cords*

And she brings news, and every tongue that speaks
But Romeo's name speaks heavenly eloquence.
Now, Nurse, what news? What hast thou there?
The cords that Romeo did bid thee fetch?   35

NURSE   Ay, ay, the cords.

JULIET   Ay me, what news? Why dost thou wring thy hands?

NURSE   Ah well a-day, he's dead, he's dead, he's dead!
We are undone, lady, we are undone.
Alack the day, he's gone, he's killed, he's dead.   40

JULIET   Can heaven be so envious?

NURSE   Romeo can,
Though heaven cannot. O Romeo, Romeo,
Who ever would have thought it? Romeo!

JULIET   What devil art thou that dost torment me thus?   45
This torture should be roared in dismal hell.
Hath Romeo slain himself? Say thou but "Ay,"
And that bare vowel "I" shall poison more
Than the death-darting eye of cockatrice.
I am not I if there be such an "Ay."   50
Or those eyes shut that make thee answer "Ay."
If he be slain say "Ay," or if not, "No."
Brief sounds determine of my weal or woe.

NURSE   I saw the wound, I saw it with mine eyes—
God save the mark—here on his manly breast.   55
A piteous corse, a bloody piteous corse,

To an impatient child who has new clothes   30

But cannot wear them. Oh, here's my Nurse.

        Enter NURSE *with rope ladder*

And she brings me news, and every mention of

Romeo's name gives me such delight.

Now, Nurse, what news? What have you there?

Is that the ladder Romeo had you fetch?   35

NURSE Yes, yes, the ladder.

JULIET What news? Why are you wringing your hands?

NURSE Oh, dear. He's dead, he's dead, he's dead!

We're in trouble, miss, we're in trouble.

Oh, what a day, he's gone, he's killed, he's dead!   40

JULIET Can heaven be so jealous?

NURSE Romeo can,

Even if heaven cannot. Oh, Romeo, Romeo,

Whoever would have thought it? Romeo!

JULIET What kind of devil are you, tormenting me like this?   45

This torture is fit only for the damned in hell.

Has Romeo killed himself? Just say "Yes"

And that simple word will be more fatal to me

Than the death-darting eye of the cockatrice.

I shall cease to be me if you answer "Yes";   50

Or if his closed eyes make you answer "Yes."

If he is dead, say "Yes." If not, "No."

A single word determines my joy or woe.

NURSE I saw the wound. I saw it with my own eyes—

God help me—there on his manly chest.   55

A pitiful corpse, a bloody, pitiful corpse,

Pale, pale as ashes, all bedaubed in blood,

All in gore-blood. I swounded at the sight.

JULIET O break, my heart. Poor bankrupt, break at once.

To prison, eyes, ne'er look on liberty.   60

Vile earth to earth resign, end motion here,

And thou and Romeo press one heavy bier.

NURSE O Tybalt, Tybalt, the best friend I had,

O courteous Tybalt, honest gentleman!

That ever I should live to see thee dead!   65

JULIET What storm is this that blows so contrary?

Is Romeo slaughtered? And is Tybalt dead?

My dearest cousin, and my dearer lord?

Then dreadful trumpet, sound the general doom,

For who is living, if those two are gone?   70

NURSE Tybalt is gone, and Romeo banished.

Romeo that killed him, he is banished.

JULIET O God! Did Romeo's hand shed Tybalt's blood?

NURSE It did, it did, alas the day, it did!

JULIET O serpent heart, hid with a flowering face.   75

Did ever dragon keep so fair a cave?

Beautiful tyrant, fiend angelical,

Dove-feathered raven, wolfish-ravening lamb!   ⟩ oxymorons

Despised substance of divinest show!

Just opposite to what thou justly seem'st!   80

A damned saint, an honorable villain!

O nature, what hadst thou to do in hell

When thou didst bower the spirit of a fiend

In mortal paradise of such sweet flesh?

Pale, pale as ashes, all covered in blood—

All clotted blood. I fainted at the sight.

JULIET Oh break, my heart, poor bankrupt, break at once.

To prison, eyes, never to look at freedom. 60

Die body, and return to dust, end your life here.

Let Romeo and me make one heavy funeral bier.

NURSE Oh Tybalt, Tybalt, the best friend I had.

Oh, courteous Tybalt, honest gentleman!

That I should have lived to see you dead! 65

JULIET What kind of storm is this, with winds so contrary?

Is Romeo murdered and is Tybalt dead?

My dearest cousin and my dearer husband?

Then doomsday's trumpet sound the world's end.

Who would want to live if those two are dead? 70

NURSE Tybalt is dead and Romeo, he is banished.

Romeo killed him, so he is banished.

JULIET Oh, God! Did Romeo's hand shed Tybalt's blood?

NURSE It did, it did, alas the day, it did.

JULIET His handsome face hid a serpent's heart. 75

Did ever a dragon own so fine a cave?

Beautiful tyrant and angelic fiend,

White feathered raven, wolf-like, devouring lamb!

Vile creature that seems so beautiful outside!

The exact opposite of what you seemed to be. 80

A sinning saint, an honorable villain!

Oh, nature, what were you doing in hell

But disguising the spirit of such a fiend

In the shape of such a handsome youth?

Was ever book containing such vile matter 85

So fairly bound? O, that deceit should dwell

In such a gorgeous palace.

NURSE There's no trust,

No faith, no honesty in men. All perjured,

All forsworn, all naught, all dissemblers. 90

Ah, where's my man? Give me some aqua vitae.

These griefs, these woes, these sorrows make me old.

Shame come to Romeo.

JULIET Blistered be thy tongue

For such a wish. He was not born to shame. 95

Upon his brow shame is ashamed to sit,

For 'tis a throne where honor may be crowned

Sole monarch of the universal earth.

O what a beast was I to chide at him.

NURSE Will you speak well of him that killed your cousin? 100

JULIET Shall I speak ill of him that is my husband?

Ah, poor my lord, what tongue shall smooth thy name?

When I thy three-hours wife have mangled it?

But wherefore, villain, didst thou kill my cousin?

That villain cousin would have killed my husband. 105

Back foolish tears, back to your native spring,

Your tributary drops belong to woe,

Which you, mistaking, offer up to joy.

My husband lives, that Tybalt would have slain,

And Tybalt's dead, that would have slain my husband. 110

All this is comfort, wherefore weep I then?

Some word there was, worser than Tybalt's death,

Was ever any book with such vile matter   85

So beautifully bound? Oh, that deceit should hide

In such a gorgeous palace.

NURSE   There's no trust,

No truth, no honesty in men. All are liars,

All are false, all are wicked, all are hypocrites.   90

Oh, where's Peter? Where's some brandy?

These griefs, these woes, these sorrows make me old.

Shame on Romeo.

JULIET   May your tongue be blistered

For such a wish. He was not born for shame.   95

Upon his brow shame is ashamed to sit,

For his brow is a throne where honor may be crowned

The only king of the entire earth.

Oh, what a beast I've been to rebuke him.

NURSE   Do you speak well of him who killed your cousin?   100

JULIET   Should I speak ill of him who is my husband?

Poor husband of mine, whose voice will praise your name

When I, your wife of three hours, muddies it?

But why, you villain, did you kill my cousin?

Because that villain cousin would have killed my husband.   105

Get back, foolish tears, to where you came from,

Your running streams belong to sorrow;

You did not know they really flowed for joy.

My husband lives, whom Tybalt would have slain,

And Tybalt's dead, who would have slain my husband.   110

All this is comforting. Why then do I weep?

Some word there was, worse than Tybalt's death,

That murdered me. I would forget it fain,
But O, it presses to my memory
Like damned guilty deeds to sinners' minds.   115
"Tybalt is dead and Romeo—banished."
That "banished," that one word "banished,"
Hath slain ten thousand Tybalts: Tybalt's death
Was woe enough, if it had ended there.
Or if sour woe delights in fellowship   120
And needly will be ranked with other griefs,
Why followed not, when she said "Tybalt's dead,"
Thy father or thy mother, nay, or both,
Which modern lamentation might have moved?
But with a rear-ward following Tybalt's death,   125
"Romeo is banished"; to speak that word
Is father, mother, Tybalt, Romeo, Juliet,
All slain, all dead. "Romeo is banished."
There is no end, no limit, measure, bound,
In that word's death. No word can that woe sound.   130
Where is my father and my mother, Nurse?
NURSE   Weeping and wailing over Tybalt's corse.
Will you go to them? I will bring you thither.
JULIET   Wash they his wounds with tears? Mine shall be spent
When theirs are dry, for Romeo's banishment.   135
Take up those cords. Poor ropes, you are beguiled,
Both you and I, for Romeo is exiled.
He made you for a highway to my bed,
But I, a maid, die a widowed virgin.
Come cords, come Nurse, I'll to my wedding bed,   140

That murdered me. I wish I could forget,

But, Oh! It weighs upon my memory,

Like damning guilty deeds on sinners' minds.   115

"Tybalt is dead and Romeo—banished!"

That "banished," that one word "banished" is like

Slaying ten thousand Tybalts. Tybalt's death

Would be bad enough if that's all there were.

If truly misery loves company,   120

And must always be joined to other griefs,

Then why not, after she said "Tybalt's dead,"

Why not also your mother or your father, or even, both?

Then normal tears would have followed.

But to follow her announcement about Tybalt   125

With "Romeo's banished," to say that word,

Is like father, mother, Tybalt, Romeo, Juliet—

All are dead. "Romeo is banished."

There is no end, no limit, no boundary to the death

That word means. No word could be worse.   130

Where are my father and my mother now, Nurse?

NURSE Weeping and wailing over Tybalt's corpse.

Will you join them? I'll take you there.

JULIET Do they wash his wounds with tears? Mine shall be spent

When theirs are dry, for Romeo's banishment.   135

Take up these cords. Poor ropes, you are beguiled,

Both you and I, for Romeo is exiled.

He made you as a ladder to my bed

But I, a maiden, die virgin-widowed.

Come ropes, come Nurse, I'll go to my wedding bed,   140

And death, not Romeo, take my maidenhead.

NURSE Hie you to your chamber. I'll find Romeo

To comfort you. I wot well where he is.

Hark ye, your Romeo will be here at night.

I'll to him. He is hid at Lawrence' cell.   145

JULIET O find him, give this ring to my true knight

And bid him come to take his last farewell.

Exeunt

Scene 3 [*Friar Lawrence' cell*]

Enter FRIAR LAWRENCE

FRIAR LAWRENCE Romeo, come forth, come forth thou
    fearful man.

Affliction is enamored of thy parts

And thou art wedded to calamity.

Enter ROMEO

ROMEO Father, what news? What is the Prince's doom?   5

What sorrow craves acquaintance at my hand

That I yet know not?

FRIAR LAWRENCE Too familiar

Is my dear son with such sour company.

I bring thee tidings of the Prince's doom.   10

ROMEO What less than doomsday is the Prince's doom?

FRIAR LAWRENCE A gentler judgement vanished from his lips:

Not body's death, but body's banishment.

ROMEO Ha! Banishment! Be merciful, say "death."

And death, not Romeo, shall take my maidenhead.

NURSE Hurry to your room. I'll find Romeo

To comfort you. I know just where he is.

Listen, your Romeo will be here tonight.

I'll find him. He is hid at the Friar's cell.   145

JULIET Oh, find him, give this ring to my true knight.

And ask him to come here to tell me farewell.

Exit

Scene 3 *[Friar Lawrence' cell]*

Enter FRIAR LAWRENCE

FRIAR LAWRENCE Come out, Romeo, come out, you

frightened fellow.

Misfortune seems to love your whole being,

And you're wedded to disaster.

Enter ROMEO

ROMEO What news, father? What is the Prince's sentence?   5

What new sorrow that I don't yet know would

Like to shake my hand?

FRIAR LAWRENCE You know

Such misfortunes all too well, dear son.

I bring you news of the Prince's sentence.   10

ROMEO What less than death has he sentenced me to?

FRIAR LAWRENCE A softer sentence issued from his lips—

Not death, but banishment.

ROMEO Banishment! Be merciful, say "death."

For exile hath more terror in his look,   15
Much more than death. Do not say "banishment."
FRIAR LAWRENCE Hence from Verona thou art banished.
Be patient, for the world is broad and wide.
ROMEO There is no world without Verona walls
But purgatory, torture, hell itself;   20
Hence "banished" is banished from the world,
And world's exile is death. Then "banished"
Is death, mistermed. Calling death "banished"
Thou cut'st my head off with a golden axe
And smilest upon the stroke that murders me.   25
FRIAR LAWRENCE O deadly sin, O rude unthankfulness.
Thy fault our law calls death, but the kind Prince,
Taking thy part hath rushed aside the law
And turned that black word "death" to banishment.
This is dear mercy and thou seest it not.   30
ROMEO 'Tis torture and not mercy. Heaven is here
Where Juliet lives, and every cat and dog
And little mouse, every unworthy thing,
Live here in heaven and may look on her,
But Romeo may not. More validity,   35
More honorable state, more courtship lives
In carrion flies than Romeo. They may seize
On the white wonder of dear Juliet's hand
And steal immortal blessing from her lips,
Who, even in pure and vestal modesty,   40
Still blush, as thinking their own kisses sin.
But Romeo may not, he is banished.

For exile has a more terrible look,   15

Much worse than death. Do not say "banishment."

FRIAR LAWRENCE Here from Verona, you are banished.

Calm down, the world is broad and wide.

ROMEO There is no world beyond Verona's walls,

Only purgatory, torture, hell itself.   20

So "banished" is banished from the world.

And exile from the world is death. Then "banished"

Is death, misnamed. Calling death "banished,"

You have cut off my head with a golden axe

And smile upon the stroke that murders me.   25

FRIAR LAWRENCE Why, what a deadly sin of rude ingratitude.

Murder's punishment is death, but the kind Prince,

Taking your side, has put aside the law

And changed that black word "death" to "banishment."

That is a great mercy, and you don't even see it.   30

ROMEO It's torture and not mercy. Heaven is here

Where Juliet lives, and every cat and dog

And little mouse, every unworthy thing

Can live here in heaven and can look at her,

But Romeo cannot. There's more value,   35

More honorable status, more courtesy even

In flies than in Romeo. They can land

On the white wonder of dear Juliet's hand

Or steal eternal bliss from her lips,

While she, in pure and maidenly modesty,   40

Still blushes and thinks it a sin when her lips touch.

But Romeo cannot; he is banished.

Flies may do this, but I from this must fly.

They are free men, but I am banished.

And say'st thou yet that exile is not death?   45

Hadst thou no poison mixed, no sharp-ground knife,

No sudden mean of death, though ne'er so mean,

But "banished" to kill me? "Banished?"

O Friar, the damned use that word in hell.

Howling attends it. How hast thou the heart,   50

Being a divine, a ghostly confessor,

A sin-absolver, and my friend professed,

To mangle me with that word "banished"?

FRIAR LAWRENCE Thou fond mad man, hear me a little speak.

ROMEO O, thou wilt speak again of banishment.   55

FRIAR LAWRENCE I'll give thee armor to keep off that word,

Adversity's sweet milk, philosophy,

To comfort thee though thou art banished.

ROMEO Yet "banished"? Hang up philosophy.

Unless philosophy can make a Juliet,   60

Displant a town, reverse a Prince's doom,

It helps not, it prevails not. Talk no more

FRIAR LAWRENCE O, then I see that mad men have no ears.

ROMEO How should they when that wise men have no eyes?

FRIAR LAWRENCE Let me dispute with thee of thy estate.   65

ROMEO Thou canst not speak of that thou dost not feel.

Wert thou as young as I, Juliet thy love,

An hour but married, Tybalt murdered,

Doting like me, and like me banished,

Then mightst thou speak, then mightst thou tear thy hair,   70

Flies can do this, but I must fly from her.

They are free men, but I am banished.

And still you say that exile is not death? 45

Have you no poison ready, no sharp-honed knife,

No means of sudden death, even if it's wrong.

But only the word "banished"? Banished?

Oh, Friar, the damned use that word in hell.

They howl at the sound of it. Have you the heart, 50

Being a priest, a spiritual confessor,

A sin-absolver, and my acknowledged friend,

To crush me with that word "banished"?

FRIAR LAWRENCE You poor foolish man. Let me speak a moment.

ROMEO Oh, you'll only speak again of banishment. 55

FRIAR LAWRENCE I'll give you a defence against that word.

I'll give you adversity's sweet milk, philosophy,

To comfort you although you have been banished.

ROMEO I'm still banished. Philosophy be hanged!

Unless philosophy can make a Juliet, 60

Can transplant a town, reverse a Prince's sentence,

It is no help, it gains nothing. Don't say anymore.

FRIAR LAWRENCE Oh, then I see that madmen have no ears.

ROMEO Why should they when wise men have no eyes?

FRIAR LAWRENCE Let's discuss your predicament. 65

ROMEO You cannot talk about what you do not feel.

If you were as young as I, and Juliet your love,

Married just an hour, Tybalt murdered,

In love as I am, and like me banished,

Then you might speak, then you might tear your hair 70

And fall upon the ground as I do now,

Taking the measure of an unmade grave.

Knocking.

FRIAR LAWRENCE Arise, one knocks. Good Romeo, hide
    thyself.

ROMEO Not I, unless the breath of heartsick groans   75

Mistlike infold me from the search of eyes.

More knocking.

FRIAR LAWRENCE Hark how they knock! Who's there?
    Romeo, arise.

Thou wilt be taken! Stay awhile! Stand up!

More knocking.

    Run to my study! By and by! God's will,   80

What simpleness is this? I come, I come!

More knocking.

    Who knocks so hard? Whence come you, what's your will?

NURSE [*Within*] Let me come in, and you shall know my errand.

I come from Lady Juliet.

FRIAR LAWRENCE Welcome then.   85

Enter NURSE

NURSE O holy Friar, O, tell me holy Friar,

Where is my lady's lord? Where's Romeo?

FRIAR LAWRENCE There on the ground, with his own tears
    made drunk.

NURSE O, he is even in my mistress' case,   90

Just in her case. O woeful sympathy,

Piteous predicament. Even so lies she,

Blubbering and weeping, weeping and blubbering.

And fall upon the ground as I do now,

Measuring the length for my grave.

Knocking.

FRIAR LAWRENCE Get up. Someone knocks. Hide

yourself, Romeo.

ROMEO No, I won't unless the mist of my heartsick groans   75

Hides me from searching eyes.

More knocking.

FRIAR LAWRENCE Listen to that knocking! Who's there?

Romeo, get up.

They'll arrest you. Wait a minute! Get up.

More knocking.

And run into my study. In a moment! God's will,   80

What silliness is this? I'm coming! I'm coming!

More knocking.

Who's knocking so hard? Where from? What do you want?

NURSE [*From within*] Let me in, and you will know my errand.

I've come from Lady Juliet.

FRIAR LAWRENCE Welcome then.   85

Enter NURSE

NURSE Oh, holy Friar, oh, tell me holy Friar,

Where is my lady's husband, where's Romeo?

FRIAR LAWRENCE There on the ground, drunk on

his own tears.

NURSE Oh, he is just like my mistress,   90

Just like her. Oh, what sympathy in sorrow,

What a terrible situation. She lies there just like that

Blubbering and weeping, weeping and blubbering.

Stand up, stand up! Stand, an you be a man!
For Juliet's sake, for her sake rise and stand!   95
Why should you fall into so deep an O?

ROMEO [*Rising*] Nurse.

NURSE Ah sir, ah sir, death's the end of all.

ROMEO Speak'st thou of Juliet? How is it with her?
Doth not she think me an old murderer,   100
Now I have stained the childhood of our joy
With blood removed but little from her own?
Where is she? And how doth she? And what says
My concealed lady to our cancelled love?

NURSE O she says nothing, sir, but weeps and weeps,   105
And now falls on her bed, and then starts up,
And Tybalt calls, and then on Romeo cries,
And then down falls again.

ROMEO As if that name,
Shot from the deadly level of a gun,   110
Did murder her, as that name's cursed hand
Murdered her kinsman. O, tell me, Friar, tell me,
In what vile part of this anatomy
Doth my name lodge? Tell me that I may sack
The hateful mansion. [*Draws his dagger*]   115

FRIAR LAWRENCE Hold thy desperate hand.
Art thou a man? Thy form cries out thou art.
Thy tears are womanish, thy wild acts denote
The unreasonable fury of a beast.
Unseemly woman in a seeming man,   120

Get up, get up, get up and be a man!

For Juliet's sake, for her sake, stand up.   95

Why should you slip into so deep an Oh-h-h?

ROMEO [*Rising*] Nurse.

NURSE Ah, sir, ah, sir, death comes to everything.

ROMEO Are you talking of Juliet? How is she?

Does she think I am just a murderer,   100

Now that I have ruined our first days together

With the slaying of her kinsman?

Where is she? How is she? And what says

My secret bride of our separated love?

NURSE Oh, she says nothing, sir, just weeps and weeps.   105

Falls first on her bed, then gets up,

Calls Tybalt's name, then calls yours,

And then falls down again.

ROMEO As if my name,

Shot from a deadly aimed gun,   110

Did murder her, as that name's cursed hand

Murdered her kinsman. Oh, tell me, Friar, tell me,

In what vile part of my body

Does my name live? Tell me so I can destroy

The hateful place. [*Draws his dagger*]   115

FRIAR LAWRENCE Stop your desperate hand!

Are you a man? You look like one,

But your tears are womanly. Your wild actions

Are like those of an unthinking beast.

You're like a raging woman in the form of a man   120

And ill-beseeming beast in seeming both!
Thou hast amazed me. By my holy order,
I thought thy disposition better tempered.
Hast thou slain Tybalt? Wilt thou slay thyself?
And slay thy lady that in thy life lives, 125
By doing damned hate upon thyself?
Why rail'st thou on thy birth, the heaven, and earth?
Since birth, and heaven, and earth, all three do meet
In thee at once; which thou at once would lose?
Fie, fie, thou sham'st thy shape, thy love, thy wit, 130
Which, like a usurer, abound'st in all,
And usest none in that true use indeed
Which should bedeck thy shape, thy love, thy wit.
Thy noble shape is but a form of wax
Digressing from the valor of a man; 135
Thy dear love sworn but hollow perjury,
Killing that love which thou hast vowed to cherish;
Thy wit, that ornament to shape and love,
Misshapen in the conduct of them both,
Like powder in a skilless soldier's flask 140
Is set afire by thine own ignorance,
And thou dismembered with thine own defence.
What, rouse thee, man! Thy Juliet is alive,
For whose dear sake thou was but lately dead.
There art thou happy. Tybalt would kill thee, 145
But thou slewest Tybalt, there are thou happy.
The law that threatened death becomes thy friend
And turns it to exile. There art thou happy.

And a monstrous beast in seeming to be both!

You astonish me. By my holy order of St. Francis,

I thought you had a better temperament than that.

Didn't you kill Tybalt? Would you kill yourself, too?

And kill the lady who loves you,   125

By damning your soul with suicide?

Why do you rail against your birth, heaven, and earth?

Since birth, heaven, and earth are combined in you,

You would lose them all in suicide.

Shame on you, you disgrace your body, your love, your mind.   130

You are like a money lender, who has countless riches

But is poor in using them,

Which should honor your body, your love, your mind.

Your noble body is a statue of wax,

Departing from the courage of a man;   135

Your sworn love is just hollow lies,

Killing the love you vowed to cherish;

Your mind that should enhance body and love

Is misused in both cases and, like gun powder

In an untrained soldier's hands,   140

Is set on fire by your own ignorance,

And you're blown apart by your own weapon.

What? Wake up man! Your Juliet is alive,

For whose dear sake you just now wanted to die.

You should be happy. Tybalt would have killed you,   145

But instead you killed him. Be happy.

The law that threatened death was friendly

And turned it to exile. Be happy.

A pack of blessings light upon thy back;

Happiness courts thee in her best array; 150

But like a misbehaved and sullen wench

Thou pouts upon thy fortune and thy love.

Take heed, take heed, for such die miserable.

Go, get thee to thy love, as was decreed,

Ascend her chamber; hence, and comfort her. 155

But look thou stay not till the watch be set,

For then thou can'st not pass to Mantua,

Where thou shalt live till we can find a time

To blaze your marriage, reconcile your friends,

Beg pardon of the Prince, and call thee back 160

With twenty hundred thousand times more joy

Then thou went'st forth in lamentation.

Go before, Nurse. Commend me to thy lady,

And bid her hasten all the house to bed,

Which heavy sorrow makes them apt unto. 165

Romeo is coming.

NURSE O Lord, I could have stayed here all the night

To hear good counsel. O what learning is!

My lord, I'll tell my lady you will come.

ROMEO Do so, and bid my sweet prepare to chide. 170

NURSE Here, sir, a ring she bid me give you, sir.

Hie you, make haste, for it grows very late.

Exit NURSE

ROMEO How well my comfort is revived by this.

FRIAR LAWRENCE Go hence, good night, and here stands all

your state: 175

Either be gone before the watch be set,

A pack of blessings alight upon your back;

Good Fortune courts you in her best array: 150

But you, like a misbehaved and sulky girl,

Complain about your lack of luck and your love.

Listen, listen, people like that die miserable.

Go, get to your love as was decided.

Climb up to her chamber, and comfort her there.   155

Be sure to leave before the curfew time,

Or you won't get away to Mantua,

Where you'll live until we can arrange

To announce your marriage, reconcile your friends,

Beg pardon of the Prince, and get you back   160

With twenty hundred thousand times more joy

Than when you left in sad regret.

Go on ahead, Nurse. Give my regards to your lady,

And tell her to urge her family to bed early.

Their sorrow will have tired them anyway.   165

Romeo is coming.

NURSE Oh lord, I could have stayed here all the night

To hear your good advice. Oh, what an education it is!

My lord, I'll tell my lady you will come.

ROMEO Do so, and tell my sweet to be ready to scold me.   170

NURSE Here, sir, is a ring she told me to give you, sir.

Hurry now, hurry, for it's getting late.

Exit NURSE

ROMEO How well my cheer is restored by this.

FRIAR LAWRENCE Off you go, good night, and here's how

things stand: 175

Either be gone before the curfew time,

Or by the break of day disguised from hence.
Sojourn in Mantua. I'll find out your man,
And he shall signify from time to time
Every good hap to you that chances here.   180
Give me thy hand. 'Tis late. Farewell. Good night.
ROMEO But that a joy past joy calls out on me,
It were a grief so brief to part with thee.
Farewell.

Exeunt

Scene 4 [*Capulet's house*]

Enter CAPULET, LADY CAPULET *and* PARIS

CAPULET Things have fallen out, sir, so unluckily,
That we have had no time to move our daughter.
Look you, she loved her kinsman Tybalt dearly,
And so did I. Well, we were born to die.
'Tis very late. She'll not come down tonight.   5
I promise you, but for your company,
I would have been abed an hour ago.
PARIS These times of woe afford no time to woo.
Madam, good night. Commend me to your daughter.
LADY CAPULET I will, and know her mind early tomorrow.   10
Tonight she's mewed up to her heaviness.
PARIS *offers to go in and* CAPULET *calls him again*
CAPULET Sir Paris, I will make a desperate tender
Of my child's love. I think she will be ruled

Or leave in disguise at break of day.

Remain in Mantua. I'll find your servant,

And he'll contact you from time to time

With any good news from here. 180

Give me your hand. It's late. Farewell. Good night.

ROMEO If a joy past all joy weren't calling me now,

I'd be sad to leave you so soon.

Farewell.

Exit

Scene 4 [*Capulet's house*]

Enter CAPULET, LADY CAPULET *and* PARIS

CAPULET Things have turned out so badly, sir,

That we've had no time to discuss this with Juliet.

You know she loved her kinsman Tybalt dearly.

And so did I. Well, we all must die sometime.

It's very late; she'll not come down tonight. 5

I assure you that if not for your company,

I would have been in bed an hour ago.

PARIS These sorrowful times allow no chance to court.

Madam, good night, give my regards to your daughter.

LADY CAPULET I will, and I'll see what she thinks tomorrow. 10

Tonight she's too wrapped up in grief.

PARIS *offers to leave, and* CAPULET *calls him back*

CAPULET Sir Paris, I will be bold and offer you

My daughter's love. I think she will be guided

In all respects by me; nay, more, I doubt it not.

Wife, go you to her ere you go to bed,   15

Acquaint her ear of my son Paris' love,

And bid her—mark you me?—on Wednesday next—

But soft—what day is this?

PARIS Monday, my lord.

CAPULET Monday! Ha ha! Well, Wednesday is too soon.   20

A Thursday let it be, a' Thursday, tell her,

She shall be married to this noble earl.

Will you be ready? Do you like this haste?

We'll keep no great ado—a friend or two.

For, hark you, Tybalt being slain so late,   25

It may be thought we held him carelessly,

Being our kinsman, if we revel much.

Therefore we'll have some half a dozen friends

And there an end. But what say you to Thursday?

PARIS My lord, I would that Thursday were tomorrow.   30

CAPULET Well, get you gone. A' Thursday be it then.

Go you to Juliet ere you go to bed,

Prepare her, wife, against this wedding day.

Farewell, my lord. Light to my chamber, ho!

Afore me, it is so very late that we   35

May call it early by and by. Good night!

Exeunt

In all things by me. In fact, I'm sure of it.

Wife, talk to her before you go to bed,   15

Tell her of friend Paris' love for her

And tell her, hear me?—on next Wednesday—

But wait, what day is this?

PARIS Monday, my lord.

CAPULET Monday! Ha, ha! Well, Wednesday is too soon.   20

Let it be Thursday, on Thursday tell her

She shall be married to this noble earl.

Will you be ready? Is that quick enough for you?

We'll make no great to-do—a friend or two,

For, remember, Tybalt's only just been slain;   25

And we don't want it thought that we held him in low regard,

Since he is our kinsman, if we celebrate too much.

We'll just have half a dozen friends in

And that's all. What do you say to Thursday?

PARIS I wish that tomorrow were Thursday.   30

CAPULET Well, goodbye then. Thursday it will be.

Wife, go to Juliet before you go to bed,

Prepare her, wife, for this wedding day.

Farewell, my lord. I need a light to get to my room.

Believe me, it is so very late that we   35

Can soon call it early. Good night.

Exit

Scene 5 [*Juliet's bedroom*]

Enter ROMEO *and* JULIET *above at the window*

JULIET Wilt thou be gone? It is not yet near day.

It was the nightingale and not the lark

That pierced the fearful hollow of thine ear.

Nightly she sings on yond pomegranate tree.

Believe me, love, it was the nightingale.   5

ROMEO It was the lark, the herald of the morn,

No nightingale. Look, love, what envious streaks

Do lace the severing clouds in yonder east.

Night's candles are burnt out, and jocund day

Stands tiptoe on the misty mountain tops.   10

I must be gone and live, or stay and die.

JULIET Yond light is not the daylight, I know it, I.

It is some meteor that the sun exhaled

To be to thee this night a torchbearer

And light thee on thy way to Mantua.   15

Therefore stay yet: thou need'st not to be gone.

ROMEO   Let me be taken, let me be put to death.

I am content, so thou wilt have it so.

I'll say yon grey is not the morning's eye,

'Tis but the pale reflex of Cynthia's brow.   20

Nor that is not the lark whose notes do beat

The vaulty heaven so high above our heads.

I have more care to stay than will to go.

Come death and welcome. Juliet wills it so.

Scene 5 [*Juliet's bedroom*]

Enter ROMEO *and* JULIET *above at the window*

JULIET Will you be going? It's not yet near dawn.

It was the nightingale and not the lark

Whose song reached your fearful ear.

She sings each night there on the pomegranate tree.

Believe me, love, it was the nightingale.   5

ROMEO It was the lark, the herald of morning,

Not the nightingale. Look, love, the jealous

Daylight streaks the clouds to the east.

Night's candles are burnt out, and cheerful day

Stands tiptoe on the misty mountain tops.   10

I must be gone and live, or stay and die.

JULIET That light is not daylight, I'm sure of that.

It's some meteor that the sun drew forth

To be this night your torchbearer

And light you on your way to Mantua.   15

Therefore, stay yet, you need not be gone.

ROMEO Let them take me, let me be put to death,

I am content if you will have it so.

I'll say that light is not the morning sun,

It's just a reflection of the moon's pale beams.   20

And that is not the lark whose notes do sound

In the arch of heaven so high above our heads.

I have more desire to stay than will to go.

Come death, you're welcome, if Juliet wills it so.

How is't, my soul? Let's talk. It is not day. 25

JULIET It is, it is. Hie hence, be gone, away.

It is the lark that sings so out of tune,

Straining harsh discords and unpleasing sharps.

Some say the lark makes sweet division;

This doth not so, for she divideth us. 30

Some say the lark and the loathed toad changed eyes.

O now I would they had changed voices too,

Since arm from arm that voice doth us affray,

Hunting thee hence with hunt's-up to the day.

O now be gone, more light and light it grows. 35

ROMEO More light and light: more dark and dark our woes.

Enter NURSE *hastily*

NURSE Madam.

JULIET Nurse?

NURSE Your lady mother is coming to your chamber.

The day is broke, be wary, look about. 40

Exit

JULIET Then, window, let day in and let life out.

ROMEO Farewell, farewell. One kiss and I'll descend.

He goes down

JULIET Art thou gone so? Love, lord, ay husband, friend?

I must hear from thee every hour in the hour,

For in a minute there are many days. 45

O, by this count I shall be much in years,

Ere I again behold my Romeo.

ROMEO Farewell!

I will omit no opportunity

Dear heart, how are you? Let's talk, for it's not dawn. 25

JULIET It is, it is. Go now, quickly, away!

It is the lark that sings so out of tune,

Voicing harsh discords and shrill sharps.

Some say the lark sings sweetly,

Not this one; she separates us. 30

Some say the lark and toad exchanged eyes.

Oh, now I wish they had changed voices too,

Since from my arms that voice tears you away,

And sends you off with a hunter's call.

Oh, now be gone! More light and light it grows. 35

ROMEO More light and light! More dark and dark our woes.

Enter NURSE

NURSE Madam.

JULIET Nurse?

NURSE Your mother is coming here to your room.

It's day break, be careful, watch out. 40

Exit NURSE

JULIET Then window, let day in and let life out!

ROMEO Farewell, farewell. One kiss, and I'll climb down.

He goes down

JULIET Have you gone? Lord, mate, yes husband, friend.

I must hear from you every hour on the hour.

For in a minute there are many days. 45

Oh, by this count, I'll have grown old

Before I see my Romeo again.

ROMEO Farewell!

I'll take each opportunity

That may convey my greetings, love, to thee.   50

JULIET O think'st thou we shall ever meet again?

ROMEO I doubt it not, and all these woes shall serve

    For sweet discourses in our times to come.

JULIET O God, I have an ill-divining soul!

    Methinks I see thee, now thou art so low,   55

    As one dead in the bottom of a tomb.

    Either my eyesight fails, or thou look'st pale.

ROMEO And trust me, love, in my eye so do you.

    Dry sorrow drinks our blood. Adieu, adieu.

Exit

JULIET O Fortune, Fortune! All men call thee fickle;   60

    If thou art fickle, what dost thou with him

    That is renowned for faith? Be fickle, Fortune,

    For then I hope thou wilt not keep him long,

    But send him back.[*She goes down from the window*]

Enter LADY CAPULET

LADY CAPULET Ho, daughter, are you up?   65

JULIET Who is't that calls? It is my lady mother.

    Is she not down so late, or up so early?

    What unaccustomed cause procures her hither?

LADY CAPULET Why, how now Juliet?

JULIET Madam, I am not well.   70

LADY CAPULET Evermore weeping for your cousin's death?

    What, wilt thou wash him from his grave with tears?

    And if thou couldst, thou couldst not make him live.

    Therefore have done. Some grief shows much of love,

To send my greetings, love, to you.   50

JULIET Do you think we'll ever meet again?

ROMEO I have no doubt. And then all these woes will make

    For sweet reminiscing in times to come.

JULIET Oh, God, I have such a dreadful fear:

    I seem to see you—as you climb below me—   55

    As dead at the bottom of a tomb.

    Either I can't see well, or you've turned pale.

ROMEO Believe me, love, in my eyes so do you.

    This sorrow drains the color. Adieu, adieu!

                         Exit ROMEO

JULIET Oh, Fortune, Fortune, all men call you fickle.   60

    If you are fickle, why do you bother with him

    Who's known for faithfulness. Be fickle, Fortune,

    For, then, perhaps you won't keep him long

    But will send him back to me. [*She goes down*]

                  Enter LADY CAPULET

LADY CAPULET Daughter! Are you up?   65

JULIET Who is it that calls? It is my dear mother.

    Is she up so late or down so early?

    What has happened to bring her here?

LADY CAPULET Are you all right, Juliet?

JULIET Madam, I am not well.   70

LADY CAPULET Forever weeping for your cousin's death?

    Come, can you wash him from his grave with tears?

    And even if you could, that would not bring him back to life.

    So, cry no more. Some grief shows your love,

But much of grief shows still some want of wit.   75

JULIET Yet let me weep for such a feeling loss.

LADY CAPULET So shall you feel the loss, but not the friend

Which you weep for.

JULIET Feeling so the loss,

I cannot choose but ever weep the friend.   80

LADY CAPULET Well, girl, thou weepst not so much for

his death

As that the villain lives which slaughtered him.

JULIET What villain, madam?

LADY CAPULET That same villain, Romeo.   85

JULIET [Aside] Villain and he be many miles asunder.

[Aloud] God pardon him. I do with all my heart.

And yet no man like he doth grieve my heart.

LADY CAPULET That is because the traitor murderer lives.

JULIET Ay madam, from the reach of these my hands.   90

Would none but I might venge my cousin's death.

LADY CAPULET We will have vengeance for it, fear thou not.

Then weep no more. I'll send to one in Mantua,

Where that same banished runagate doth live,

Shall give him such an unaccustomed dram   95

That he shall soon keep Tybalt company;

And then I hope thou wilt be satisfied.

JULIET Indeed I shall never be satisfied

With Romeo, till I behold him—dead—

Is my poor heart, so for a kinsman vexed.   100

Madam, if you could find out but a man

To bear a poison, I would temper it—

Too much grief makes you look foolish.   75

JULIET Yet, let me cry for such a deep-felt loss.

LADY CAPULET You may feel the loss, but that won't help the friend

    For whom you weep.

JULIET Feeling such a loss,

    I can't help but weep for the friend.   80

LADY CAPULET Well, my girl, you're not weeping so much for

      his death

    As that the villain lives who murdered him.

JULIET What villain, mother?

LADY CAPULET That villain, Romeo.   85

JULIET [Aside] May the villain and he be many miles away.

    [Aloud] God pardon him. I do with all my heart.

    And yet no man grieves my heart as much as he.

LADY CAPULET That is because the traitor murderer lives.

JULIET Yes, madam, beyond the reach of these hands of mine,   90

    May none but I avenge my cousin's death.

LADY CAPULET We will have vengeance for it, don't worry.

    So, weep no more. I'll ask a man in Mantua,

    Where that banished murderer now lives,

    And he'll give him a special drink   95

    So that he'll soon keep Tybalt company.

    And then I hope you will be satisfied.

JULIET Indeed, I never will be satisfied

    With Romeo until I see him again—dead—

    Such is my poor heart to think of a kinsman killed.   100

    Madam, if you could find a man

    To bring that poison, I would mix it

That Romeo should upon receipt thereof
Soon sleep in quiet. O, how my heart abhors
To hear him named, and cannot come to him, 105
To wreak the love I bore my cousin
Upon his body that hath slaughtered him.
LADY CAPULET Find thou the means, and I'll find such a man.
But now I'll tell thee joyful tidings, girl.
JULIET And joy comes well in such a needy time. 110
What are they, I beseech your ladyship?
LADY CAPULET Well, well, thou hast a careful father, child;
One who to put thee from thy heaviness
Hath sorted out a sudden day of joy,
That thou expects not, nor I looked not for. 115
JULIET Madam, in happy time. What day is that?
LADY CAPULET Marry, my child, early next Thursday morn,
The gallant, young, and noble gentleman,
The County Paris, at St. Peter's Church,
Shall happily make thee there a joyful bride. 120
JULIET Now by St. Peter's Church, and Peter too,
He shall not make me there a joyful bride.
I wonder at this haste, that I must wed
Ere he that should be husband comes to woo.
I pray you tell my lord and father, madam, 125
I will not marry yet. And when I do, I swear
It shall be Romeo, whom you know I hate,
Rather than Paris. These are news indeed!
LADY CAPULET Here comes your father, tell him so yourself,
And see how he will take it at your hands. 130

So that Romeo would, when he drank it,

Soon sleep in peace. Oh, how my heart hates

To hear him named when I cannot reach him 105

To satisfy the love I felt for my cousin

Upon his body, he who murdered him.

LADY CAPULET Get the poison, and I'll get the man to carry it.

But now, I'll tell you some joyful news, my girl.

JULIET Good news is certainly welcome at such a time. 110

What is it, mother dear?

LADY CAPULET Well, well, you have a caring father, my child.

One who, to free you from your heavy heart,

Has chosen a day of joy in the near future

That you did not expect, nor did I look for. 115

JULIET Madam, such perfect timing, what day is that?

LADY CAPULET Well, my child, early next Thursday morning

The gallant, young, and noble gentleman,

The Count Paris, at St. Peter's Church

Will happily make you there a joyful bride. 120

JULIET Now, by St. Peter's Church, and Peter, too,

He shall not make me there a joyful bride.

Why is there such a hurry, that I must wed

Before my future husband even comes to woo?

Mother, please tell my lord and father 125

That I will not marry yet. And when I wed, I swear

It shall be Romeo, whom you know I hate,

Rather than Paris. Such news indeed!

LADY CAPULET Here comes your father, tell him so yourself

And see how he will take this news from you. 130

Enter CAPULET *and* NURSE

CAPULET When the sun sets, the earth doth drizzle dew,

But for the sunset of my brother's son,

It rains downright.

How now, a conduit, girl? What, still in tears?

Evermore showering? In one little body   135

Thou counterfeits a bark, a sea, a wind.

For still thy eyes, which I may call the sea,

Do ebb and flow with tears. The bark thy body is,

Sailing in this salt flood, the winds thy sighs,

Who raging with thy tears, and they with them,   140

Without a sudden calm will overset

Thy tempest-tossed body. How now, wife?

Have you delivered to her our decree?

LADY CAPULET Ay sir, but she will none, she gives you thanks.

I would the fool were married to her grave.   145

CAPULET Soft. Take me with you, take me with you, wife.

How! Will she none! Doth she not give us thanks?

Is she not proud? Doth she not count her blest,

Unworthy as she is, that we have wrought

So worthy a gentleman to be her bride?   150

JULIET Not proud you have, but thankful that you have.

Proud can I never be of what I hate,

But thankful even for hate that is meant love.

CAPULET How, how, how, how? Chopped logic? What is this?

"Proud" and "I thank you" and "I thank you not"   155

And yet "not proud"? Mistress minion you,

Thank me no thankings nor proud me no prouds,

Enter CAPULET *and* NURSE

CAPULET When the sun sets, the earth sheds drops of dew,

But for the sunset of my brother's son,

It pours rain.

What now, a girl-fountain? What, still in tears,

Always gushing in one little body?   135

You remind me of a boat, a sea, a wind;

Your eyes, which I'll call the sea,

Do ebb and flow with tears. Your body, the boat,

Sails on the salt flood; your sighs, the wind,

Rage with your tears, and they with them,   140

And unless there's a sudden calm, you'll overturn

The storm-tossed boat, your body. Well, wife,

Have you told her what we plan for her?

LADY CAPULET Yes, sir, but she says no thanks to it.

I wish the silly girl were married to her grave!   145

CAPULET Wait a bit, I don't follow you, wife.

How do you mean "no thanks"? She doesn't thank us?

Isn't she honored? Doesn't she count herself blessed,

Unworthy as she is, that we've arranged

For such a worthy gentleman to be her bridegroom?   150

JULIET Not honored that you have, but grateful that you have.

I can never be honored by what I hate.

But I'm grateful for what is meant to show your love.

CAPULET What is this? Such quibbling with words. What is this?

Honored and grateful, but no thanks?   155

And yet not honored. You spoiled child!

Thank me no thanks and honor me no honors,

But fettle your fine joints 'gainst Thursday next

To go with Paris to St. Peter's Church,

Or I will drag thee on a hurdle thither. 160

Out, you green-sickness carrion! Out, you baggage!

You tallow-face!

LADY CAPULET Fie, fie. What, are you mad?

JULIET Good father, I beseech you on my knees.

Hear me with patience but to speak a word. 165

CAPULET Hang thee young baggage, disobedient wretch!

I tell thee what—get thee to church a Thursday

Or never after look me in the face.

Speak not, reply not, do not answer me.

My fingers itch. Wife, we scarce thought us blest 170

That God had lent us but this only child;

But now I see this one is one too much,

And that we have a curse in having her.

Out on her, hilding.

NURSE God in heaven bless her. 175

You are to blame, my lord, to rate her so.

CAPULET And why, my Lady Wisdom? Hold your tongue,

Good Prudence! Smatter with your gossips, go.

NURSE I speak no treason.

CAPULET O God, ye god-den! 180

NURSE May not one speak?

CAPULET Peace, you mumbling fool!

Utter your gravity o'er a gossip's bowl,

For here we need it not.

LADY CAPULET You are too hot. 185

Just get your worthless carcass ready for next Thursday.

Go with Paris to St. Peter's Church,

Or I will drag you there on a hangman's cart. 160

Now get out, green-faced corpse. Out, you slut,

You pale-faced wretch.

LADY CAPULET Wait! Wait! Are you crazy?

JULIET Good father, I ask you on my knees,

Be patient while I explain. 165

CAPULET Hang you, young slut, disobedient wretch.

I'll tell you what—get to church on Thursday

Or never again look me in the face.

Don't speak, don't answer me back.

My fingers itch to slap you. Wife, we were barely blessed, 170

We thought, when God gave us just this child,

But now I see this one is one too many,

And that we have been cursed in having her.

Out with her, good-for-nothing creature.

NURSE God in heaven bless her. 175

You are wrong, my lord, to condemn her so.

CAPULET And why is that, Lady-Know-It-All? Hold your tongue!

Mistress Careful. Go gossip with your old cronies!

NURSE I'm not being disloyal—

CAPULET Oh, God, good day! 180

NURSE May one not speak?

CAPULET Quiet, you mumbling fool,

Save your lecture for your table gossip.

We don't want it here.

LADY CAPULET You are too angry. 185

CAPULET God's bread, it makes me mad!
    Day, night, hour, tide, time, work, play,
    Alone, in company, still my care hath been
    To have her matched. And having now provided
    A gentleman of noble parentage,   190
    Of fair demesnes, youthful and nobly ligned,
    Stuffed, as they say, with honorable parts,
    Proportioned as one's thought would wish a man—
    And then to have a wretched puling fool,
    A whining mammet, in her fortune's tender,   195
    To answer "I'll not wed, I cannot love,
    I am too young, I pray you pardon me!"
    But, an you will not wed, I'll pardon you!
    Graze where you will, you shall not house with me.
    Look to't, think on't, I do not use to jest.   200
    Thursday is near. Lay hand on heart. Advise.
    An you be mine I'll give you to my friend;
    An you be not, hang! Beg! Starve! Die in the streets!
    For by my soul I'll ne'er acknowledge thee,
    Not what is mine shall never do thee good.   205
    Trust to 't, bethink you. I'll not be forsworn.
                            He exits

JULIET Is there no pity sitting in the clouds
    That sees into the bottom of my grief?
    O sweet my mother, cast me not away,
    Delay this marriage for a month, a week,   210
    Or if you do not, make the bridal bed
    In that dim monument where Tybalt lies.

CAPULET By God's bread, it makes me mad.

    Day and night, every hour and season, at work or play

    Alone or with others, my concern was always

    To have her married. And now having provided

    A gentleman of noble parentage,   190

    Of large estates, young and well brought up,

    Full, as they say, of honorable traits,

    Well-built as one would wish a man to be,

    And then to have some wretched puking fool,

    A whining crybaby, at such good fortune,   195

    Answer, "I'll not wed, I cannot love,

    I'm too young, please excuse me!"

    If you don't wed, just see if I'll excuse you!

    Get your meals where you can, not in my house.

    See about it. Think it over. I'm not joking.   200

    Thursday is near. Look in your heart. Consider it.

    As you are my daughter, I can give you in marriage.

    If not, then go hang, beg, starve, die in the street

    For I swear, I'll never acknowledge you,

    And nothing of what I own shall ever go to you.   205

    Think it over. Believe me, I won't change my mind.

                               He exits

JULIET Is there no pity dwelling in heaven

    That sees to the depth of my grief?

    Oh, dearest mother, don't cast me aside.

    Delay this marriage for a month, a week,   210

    Or if you will not, make my bridal bed

    In that dark tomb where Tybalt lies.

LADY CAPULET Talk not to me, for I'll not speak a word.

    Do as thou wilt, for I have done with thee.

Exit

JULIET O God! O Nurse, how shall this be prevented?   215

    My husband is on earth, my faith in heaven.

    How shall that faith return again to earth,

    Unless that husband send it me from heaven

    By leaving earth? Comfort me, counsel me.

    Alack, alack, that heaven should practice stratagems   220

    Upon so soft a subject as myself!

    What sayest thou? Hast thou not a word of joy?

    Some comfort, Nurse.

NURSE Faith, here it is.

    Romeo is banished, and all the world to nothing   225

    That he dares ne'er come back to challenge you.

    Or if he do, it needs must be by stealth.

    Then, since the case so stands as now it doth,

    I think it best you married with the County.

    O he's a lovely gentleman!   230

    Romeo's a dishclout to him. An eagle, madam,

    Hath not so green, so quick, so fair an eye

    As Paris hath. Beshrew my very heart,

    I think you are happy in this second match,

    For it excels your first; or, if it did not,   235

    Your first is dead, or 'twere as good he were

    As living here and you no use of him.

JULIET Speakest thou from thy heart?

NURSE And from my soul too, else beshrew them both.

JULIET Amen.   240

LADY CAPULET Don't talk to me because I won't answer.

    Do as you wish, for I'm through with you.

                        Exit LADY CAPULET

JULIET Oh God. Oh, nurse. How can I stop this?   215

    My husband is alive; heaven knows I'm married.

    How can anything change that

    Unless my husband dies and leaves this earth?

    Oh, comfort me, Nurse, advise me.

    Oh, dear, that heaven should play such tricks   220

    Upon such a weak creature as I.

    What do you say? Nothing to cheer me?

    Give me some comfort, Nurse.

NURSE Well, here it is.

    Romeo is banished, and there's no chance in the world   225

    That he dares come back to claim you as his wife.

    Or if he does, it will have to be secretly.

    So, as things stand for now,

    I think it's best you marry Count Paris.

    Oh, he's a lovely gentleman.   230

    Romeo's a dishcloth compared to him. An eagle, madam,

    Has not so green or quick or fair an eye

    As Paris has. Curse me if I'm wrong, but

    I think you're lucky in this second match,

    For it excels your first; or even if not,   235

    Your first one's dead, or might as well be,

    Since he's alive but can't be here with you.

JULIET Do you speak from your heart?

NURSE And from my soul too, or else curse them both.

JULIET Amen.   240

NURSE   What?

JULIET   Well, thou hast comforted me marvelous much.

Go in, and tell my lady I am gone,

Having displeased my father, to Lawrence' cell,

To make confession and to be absolved.   245

NURSE   Marry, I will; and this is wisely done.

Exit

JULIET   Ancient damnation! O most wicked fiend!

Is it more sin to wish me thus forsworn,

Or to dispraise my lord with that same tongue

Which she hath praised him with above compare   250

So many thousand times? Go, counsellor.

Thou and my bosom henceforth shall be twain.

I'll to the friar to know his remedy.

If all else fail, myself have power to die.

Exit

> speaking about nurse

NURSE What?

JULIET Well, you've been an enormous comfort to me.

Go in and tell my mother I've gone—

Having displeased my father—to Lawrence' cell

To make my confession and be absolved.   245

NURSE Indeed, I will. And this is wise to do.

Exit NURSE

JULIET You old devil! You wicked fiend!

Is she more sinful to urge me to break my vows

Or to insult my husband with the same tongue

That she used to praise him as beyond compare   250

So many thousand times? Go, counselor,

I'll never trust you again with my heart's secrets.

I'll ask the friar what I should do.

If all else fails, then I can always kill myself.

Exit

Act Four

Enter FRIAR LAWRENCE *and* PARIS

FRIAR LAWRENCE On Thursday, sir? The time is very short.

PARIS My father Capulet will have it so,

    And I am nothing slow to slack his haste.

FRIAR LAWRENCE You say you do not know the lady's mind.

    Uneven is the course. I like it not.   5

PARIS Immoderately she weeps for Tybalt's death,

    And therefore have I little talked of love,

    For Venus smiles not in a house of tears.

    Now sir, her father counts it dangerous

    That she do give her sorrow so much sway,   10

    And in his wisdom hastes our marriage

    To stop the inundation of her tears,

    Which, too much minded by herself alone,

    May be put from her by society.

    Now do you know the reason of this haste.   15

FRIAR LAWRENCE [*Aside*] I would I knew not why it should be slowed.

    Look sir, here comes the lady toward my cell.

Enter JULIET

PARIS Happily met, my lady and my wife.

JULIET That may be, sir, when I may be a wife.

PARIS That "may be" must be, love, on Thursday next.   20

JULIET What must be, shall be.

Act Four

Enter FRIAR LAWRENCE *and* PARIS

FRIAR LAWRENCE On Thursday, sir? That's very sudden.

PARIS Her father, Capulet, wants it so.

And I'm not someone who'd hold him back.

FRIAR LAWRENCE You say you don't know how the lady feels.

This is irregular. I don't like it.   5

PARIS She's crying constantly over Tybalt's death.

And so I've had little chance to court her,

For love smiles not in a house of tears.

Now, sir, her father thinks it dangerous

That she's affected so deeply by this sorrow,   10

And in his wisdom hastens our marriage

To stop the overflowing of her tears

Which, now that she is left alone so much,

Requires that she have some company.

And now you know the reason for this haste.   15

FRIAR LAWRENCE [*Aside*] I wish I had a reason to postpone it.

Look, sir, here comes the lady toward my cell.

Enter JULIET

PARIS Well met, my lady, and my wife!

JULIET That may be, sir, when I can be a wife.

PARIS That "may be" must be, love, on next Thursday.   20

JULIET What must be, shall be.

FRIAR LAWRENCE That's a certain text.

PARIS Come you to make confession to this father?

JULIET To answer that, I should confess to you.

PARIS Do not deny to him that you love me.   25

JULIET I will confess to you that I love him.

PARIS So will ye, I am sure, that you love me.

JULIET If I do so, it will be of more price,

    Being spoke behind your back, than to your face.

PARIS Poor soul, thy face is much abused with tears.   30

JULIET The tears have got small victory by that,

    For it was bad enough before their spite.

PARIS Thou wrong'st it more than tears with that report.

JULIET That is no slander, sir, which is a truth,

    And what I spake, I spake it to my face.   35

PARIS Thy face is mine, and thou hast slandered it.

JULIET It may be so, for it is not mine own.

    Are you at leisure, holy father, now,

    Or shall I come to you at evening Mass?

FRIAR LAWRENCE My leisure serves me, pensive daughter, now.   40

    My lord, we must entreat the time alone.

PARIS God shield I should disturb devotion!

    Juliet, on Thursday early will I rouse ye.

    Till then, adieu, and keep this holy kiss.

                                 Exit PARIS

JULIET O shut the door! and when thou hast done so,   45

    Come weep with me, past hope, past care, past help!

FRIAR LAWRENCE O Juliet, I already know thy grief;

FRIAR LAWRENCE That's a true saying.

PARIS Have you come here to make confession to this father?

JULIET If I answered that, I'd be confessing to you.

PARIS Don't tell him you don't love me.   25

JULIET I will confess to you that I love him.

PARIS You'll also confess, I'm sure, that you love me.

JULIET If I do, it will mean much more,

    Being said behind your back, than to your face.

PARIS Poor dear, your face is stained with tears.   30

JULIET The tears don't change much.

    My face was bad enough before.

PARIS You wrong it more than tears with that remark.

JULIET I spoke no slander, sir, it's the truth,

    And what I said, I said to my face.   35

PARIS Your face is mine, and you have slandered it.

JULIET That may be true, for it's not my own.

    Are you free now, holy father,

    Or shall I come back at evening Mass?

FRIAR LAWRENCE I have the time right now, sad daughter.   40

    My lord, I must ask you to give us time to be alone.

PARIS God forbid I should disturb prayers.

    Juliet, I'll waken you, early Thursday.

    Till then, adieu, and hold this holy kiss.

                              Exit PARIS

JULIET Oh, shut the door, and when you've done that   45

    Come weep with me for I'm past hope, past care, past help!

FRIAR LAWRENCE Oh, Juliet, I understand your grief.

It strains me past the compass of my wits.

I hear thou must—and nothing may prorogue it—

On Thursday next be married to this County. 50

JULIET Tell me not, Friar, that thou hearest of this,

Unless thou tell me how I may prevent it.

If in thy wisdom thou canst give no help,

Do thou but call my resolution wise,

And with this knife I'll help it presently. 55

God joined my heart and Romeo's, thou our hands;

And ere this hand, by thee to Romeo's sealed,

Shall be the label to another deed,

Or my true heart with treacherous revolt

Turn to another, this shall slay them both. 60

Therefore, out of thy long-experienced time

Give me some present counsel, or behold:

'Twixt my extremes and me, this bloody knife

Shall play the umpire, arbitrating that

Which the commission of thy years and art 65

Could to no issue of true honor bring.

Be not so long to speak. I long to die

If what thou speak'st speak not of remedy.

FRIAR LAWRENCE Hold, daughter. I do spy a kind of hope

Which craves as desperate an execution 70

As that is desperate which we would prevent.

If, rather than to marry County Paris,

Thou hast the strength of will to slay thyself,

Then is it likely thou wilt undertake

A thing like death to chide away this shame, 75

It pushes me beyond my wit's end.

I hear you must—and nothing can postpone it—

On Thursday next be married to this count. 50

JULIET Don't tell me, Friar, that you've heard this,

Unless you can tell me how to prevent it.

If with all your wisdom you can't help me,

Then tell me that which I must do is wise,

And with this knife, I'll solve the problem now. 55

God joined my heart and Romeo's; you, our hands.

Before this hand, which you with vows gave Romeo,

Shall sign another contract in marriage,

Or my true heart would in treacherous revolt

Turn to another, this hand will slay them both. 60

Therefore, out of your many years' experience,

Give me some good advice, or behold—

Between my problems and me this deadly knife

Will play the umpire, deciding that

Which all the judgment of your years and wisdom 65

Could not resolve in an honorable way.

Don't take too long to speak. I long to die

If your reply contains no remedy.

FRIAR LAWRENCE Wait, daughter! I see a ray of hope

Which requires an action as dangerous 70

As the danger we seek to avoid.

If, rather than marry Count Paris,

You have the courage to kill yourself,

Then it is probable you dare to risk

Something like death to avoid this disgrace, 75

> tells her
his plan

That cop'st with death himself to 'scape from it.
And if thou dar'st, I'll give thee remedy.

JULIET O bid me leap, rather than marry Paris,
 From off the battlements of any tower,
 Or walk in thievish ways, or bid me lurk   80
 Where serpents are. Chain me with roaring bears,
 Or hide me nightly in a charnel-house
 O'ercovered quite with dead men's rattling bones,
 With reeky shanks and yellow chapless skulls.
 Or bid me go into a new-made grave,   85
 And hide me with a dead man in his shroud—
 Things that, to hear them told, have made me tremble—
 And I will do it without fear or doubt.
 To live an unstained wife to my sweet love.

FRIAR LAWRENCE Hold then. Go home, be merry, give consent 90
 To marry Paris. Wednesday is tomorrow;
 Tomorrow night look that thou lie alone.
 Let not the Nurse lie with thee in thy chamber.
 Take thou this vial, being then in bed,
 And this distilling liquor drink thou off;   95
 When presently through all thy veins shall run
 A cold and drowsy humor, for no pulse
 Shall keep his native progress, but surcease.
 No warmth, no breath shall testify thou livest,
 The roses in thy lips and cheeks shall fade   100
 To paly ashes, thy eyes' windows fall,
 Like death when he shuts up the day of life.
 Each part deprived of supple government,

If you would face Death himself to escape from it.

If you have the courage, I have a solution.

JULIET Oh, tell me to leap, rather than marry Paris,

From off the battlements of any tower,

Or to walk among thieves, or tell me to lie   80

Where snakes nest. Chain me with roaring bears,

Or hide me nightly in a morgue

All covered up with dead men's rattling bones,

With stinking limbs and yellow jawless skulls.

Ask me to lie in a newly dug grave,   85

And hide me with a dead man in his shroud—

Things that to hear them told have made me tremble—

I'll now do without fear or doubt

To live as faithful wife to my sweet love.

FRIAR LAWRENCE Take heart. Go home, be cheerful,   90

Agree to marry Paris. Tomorrow is Wednesday.

Tomorrow night be sure to sleep alone.

Don't let the Nurse sleep with you in your room.

Take this little bottle, when you're in bed,

Drink the distilled liquor it holds right down.   ⟩ Lawrence's 95

Then soon after, through all your veins will run   Plan

A cold and drowsy feeling, for no pulse

Will keep beating normally, but cease.

No warmth or breath will show that you still live.

The roses in your lips and cheeks will fade   100

To a pale ashy color. Your eyelids will close,

Like death when ending up the day of life.

Your limbs, deprived of movement,

Shall stiff and stark and cold appear, like death,
And in this borrowed likeness of shrunk death   105
Thou shalt continue two and forty hours,
And then awake as from a pleasant sleep.
Now when the bridegroom in the morning comes
To rouse thee from thy bed, there thou art, dead.
Then, as the manner of our country is,   110
In thy best robes, uncovered on the bier   > plan
Thou shall be borne to that same ancient vault,
Where all the kindred of the Capulets lie.
In the meantime, against thou shalt awake,
Shall Romeo by my letters know our drift,   115
And hither shall he come; and he and I
Will watch thy waking, and that very night
Shall Romeo bear thee hence to Mantua.
And this shall free thee from this present shame,
If no inconstant toy nor womanish fear   120
Abate thy valor in the acting it.
JULIET Give me, give me! O tell me not of fear.
FRIAR LAWRENCE Hold. Get you gone. Be strong and prosperous
    In this resolve. I'll send a friar with speed
    To Mantua with my letters to thy lord.   125
JULIET Love give me strength, and strength shall help afford.
    Farewell, dear father.

                        Exit

Shall stiff and stark and cold appear, like death.

And in this false likeness of death, 105

You will lie for forty-two hours,

And then you'll awake as from a pleasant sleep.

Now when the groom comes in the morning

To awaken you from sleep, there you are, dead.

Then, as is the custom in this country, 110

You'll be placed in your best clothes upon a bier

And carried to the same ancient tomb

Where all the kinsmen of the Capulets lie.

Meanwhile, against the time when you will awake

My letter will reach Romeo to tell him our plan 115

And he'll come here; then he and I

Will watch for you to wake, and that same night

Will you be taken by Romeo on to Mantua;

And that will free you from this shameful dilemma,

Providing no change of mind or girlish fear 120

Takes away your courage in the process.

JULIET Just give the bottle to me and don't talk of fear.

FRIAR LAWRENCE Here, take it. Go. Be strong and have success

In this resolve. I'll send a friar with speed

To Mantua with my letter to your husband. 125

JULIET Love, give me strength, and strength will help me through.

Farewell, dear father.

Exit

185

Scene 2 [*Capulet's house*]

Enter CAPULET, LADY CAPULET, NURSE, *and two or three* SERVANTS

CAPULET So many guests invite as here are writ.

Exit SERVANT

Sirrah, go hire me twenty cunning cooks.

SERVANT You shall have none ill, sir, for I'll try if they can lick
their fingers.

CAPULET How canst thou try them so?   5

SERVANT Marry, sir, 'tis an ill cook that cannot lick his own
fingers; therefore he that cannot lick his fingers goes not
with me.

CAPULET Go, be gone.

Exit SERVANT

We shall be much unfurnished for this time.   10

What, is my daughter gone to Friar Lawrence?

NURSE Ay, forsooth.

CAPULET Well, he may chance to do some good on her.

A peevish self-willed harlotry it is.

Enter JULIET

NURSE See where she comes from shrift with merry look.   15

CAPULET How now, my headstrong: where have you
been gadding?

JULIET Where I have learnt me to repent the sin
Of disobedient opposition
To you and your behests, and am enjoined   20

Scene 2 [*Capulet's house*]

Enter CAPULET, LADY CAPULET, NURSE, *and two or three* SERVANTS

CAPULET Invite all the guests here on this list.

Exit SERVANT

And you, hire me twenty talented cooks.

SERVANT You'll have the best, sir. I'll test them to see if they can

lick their fingers.

CAPULET What kind of test is that?   5

SERVANT Why sir, it's a bad cook who won't lick his fingers.

I won't hire any who doesn't like his own cooking

that much.

CAPULET Oh, go on.

Exit SERVANT

We're not going to be ready in time.   10

What, has my daughter gone to Friar Lawrence?

NURSE Yes, sir.

CAPULET Well, he may perhaps do some good with her,

Peevish, headstrong, foolish wench that she is.

Enter JULIET

NURSE See how she returns from confession with a smile.   15

CAPULET Well now, my stubborn girl, where have you been

gadding about?

JULIET Where I have learned to repent my sin

Of disobedient opposition

To you and your commands and am urged   20

By holy Lawrence to fall prostrate here,

To beg your pardon. Pardon, I beseech you.

Henceforward I am ever ruled by you.

CAPULET Send for the County, go tell him of this.

I'll have this knot knit up tomorrow morning. >changes   25
done

JULIET I met the youthful lord at Lawrence' cell,

And gave him what becomed love I might,

Not stepping o'er the bounds of modesty.

CAPULET Why I am glad on't. This is well. Stand up.

This is as 't should be. Let me see the County.   30

Ay, marry. Go, I say, and fetch him hither.

Now afore God, this reverend holy friar,

All our whole city is much bound to him.

JULIET Nurse, will you go with me into my closet,

To help me sort such needful ornaments   35

As you think fit to furnish me tomorrow?

LADY CAPULET No, not till Thursday, there is time enough.

CAPULET Go, Nurse, go with her. We'll to church

tomorrow.

Exit JULIET *and* NURSE

LADY CAPULET We shall be short in our provision,   40

'Tis now near night.

CAPULET 'Tush, I will stir about,

And all things shall be well. I warrant thee, wife,

Go thou to Juliet, help to deck up her.

I'll not to bed tonight. Let me alone.   45

Exit LADY CAPULET

I'll play the housewife for this once. What ho!

By holy Lawrence to kneel at your feet

To beg your pardon. Pardon me, I beg you.

From now on I will be ruled by you.

CAPULET Send for Count Paris, go tell him of this.

I'll tie this wedding knot tomorrow morning.   25

JULIET I met the young lord at Lawrence's cell,

And gave him such affection as was fit,

Not overstepping the bounds of modesty.

CAPULET Why, I'm glad to hear it. Good. Stand up.

This is all as it should be. Let me see the Count.   30

Yes, good. Go and bring him to me.

Now, before God, this whole city has cause

To be grateful to Friar Lawrence.

JULIET Nurse, will you go with me to my room

To help me choose such needed clothes and things   35

As you think I should wear tomorrow?

LADY CAPULET No, not till Thursday. There's time enough.

CAPULET Go, Nurse, go with her. We'll go to church

tomorrow early.

Exit NURSE *and* JULIET

LADY CAPULET We'll be short of provisions—   40

It's almost night now.

CAPULET Hush, now, I'll get busy,

And all will turn out well, I promise, wife.

You go to Juliet and help to deck her out.

I won't go to bed tonight. Leave it all to me.   45

Exit LADY CAPULET

I'll play the housewife this once. Hey there!

They are all forth. Well, I will walk myself

To County Paris, to prepare up him

Against tomorrow. My heart is wondrous light

Since this same wayward girl is so reclaimed.   50

Exeunt

Scene 3 [*Juliet's bedroom*]

Enter JULIET *and* NURSE

JULIET Ay, these attires are best. But, gentle Nurse,

I pray thee leave me to myself tonight,

For I have need of many orisons

To move the heavens to smile upon my state,

Which, well thou knowest, is cross and full of sin.   5

Enter LADY CAPULET

LADY CAPULET What, are you busy, ho? Need you my help?

JULIET No madam. We have culled such necessaries

As are behoveful for our state tomorrow.

So please you, let me now be left alone,

And let the Nurse this night sit up with you,   10

For I am sure you have your hands full all

In this so sudden business.

LADY CAPULET Good night.

Get thee to bed and rest, for thou hast need.

Exit LADY CAPULET *and* NURSE

JULIET Farewell. God knows when we shall meet again.   15

I have a faint cold fear thrills through my veins,

That almost freezes up the heat of life.

They've all gone out. Well, I'll walk to see
Count Paris myself, to prepare him for
Tomorrow. My heart is much lighter
Since this same wayward girl is so subdued.   50

Exit

Scene 3 [*Juliet's room*]

Enter JULIET *and* NURSE

JULIET Yes, these clothes will do. But, gentle Nurse,
Please leave me by myself tonight.
For I will need to offer many prayers
To move heaven to smile upon my frame of mind,
Which, as you well know, is quarrelsome and full of sin.   5

Enter LADY CAPULET

LADY CAPULET Well, are you busy here? Do you need my help?

JULIET No, madam. We have found what is needed
To be properly dressed for tomorrow.
So, please, just let me be left alone now,
And have the Nurse stay with you tonight,   10
For I'm sure you have your hands quite full
In this so hurried up affair.

LADY CAPULET Good night.
Get to bed and rest, for you'll need it.

Exit LADY CAPULET *and* NURSE

JULIET Farewell. God knows when we shall meet again.   15
I feel a chilling fear that runs through my blood
That almost freezes up the heat of life.

I'll call them back again to comfort me.
Nurse! What should she do here?
My dismal scene I needs must act alone.   20
Come vial.
What if this mixture do not work at all?
Shall I be married then tomorrow morning?
No, no. This shall forbid it. [*She lays down her knife*]
Lie thou there.   25
What if it be a poison which the friar
Subtly hath ministered to have me dead,
Lest in this marriage he should be dishonored,
Because he married me before to Romeo?
I fear it is; and yet methinks it should not,   30
For he hath still been tried a holy man.
How if, when I am laid into the tomb,
I wake before the time that Romeo
Come to redeem me? There's a fearful point!
Shall I not then be stifled in the vault,   35
To whose foul mouth no healthsome air breathes in,
And there die strangled ere my Romeo comes?
Or, if I live, is it not very like,
The horrible conceit of death and night,
Together with the terror of the place—   40
As in a vault, an ancient receptacle,
Where, for this many hundred years, the bones
Of all my buried ancestors are packed;
Where bloody Tybalt yet but green in earth,
Lies festering in his shroud; where, as they say,   45

I'll call them back again to comfort me.

Nurse! But what could she do?

I must act alone in this grim business.   20

Come, little bottle.

But what if this mixture doesn't work at all?

Shall I be married tomorrow morning?

No, this dagger will prevent that. [*She lays down a dagger*]

Lie right here.   25

What if this is a poison that the friar

Has subtly provided to have me die,

So he won't be dishonored by this marriage,

Since he has already married me to Romeo?

I'm afraid it is, but then I know it couldn't be—   30

For the friar has always proved to be a holy man.

What if, when I'm laid in the tomb,

I awake before the time that Romeo

Arrives to rescue me? What a frightening thought!

Won't I then be smothered in the tomb,   35

Through whose foul mouth no wholesome air comes in,

And there I'll die choked before my Romeo comes?

Or if I live, isn't it likely that

Thoughts of death and darkest night,

Together with the terror of the place—   40

Which is a vault, an ancient burial place,

Where for these many hundred years the bones

Of all my buried ancestors are stacked;

Where bloody Tybalt yet so new in earth

Lies rotting in his shroud; where, they say   45

At some hours in the night spirits resort—
Alack, alack! Is it not like that I,
So early waking, what with loathsome smells
And shrieks like mandrakes torn out of the earth,
That living mortals, hearing them run mad— 50
O if I wake, shall I not be distraught,
Environed with all these hideous fears,
And madly play with my forefathers' joints,
And pluck the mangled Tybalt from his shroud
And, in this rage, with some great kinsman's bone, 55
As with a club, dash out my desperate brains?
O look! Methinks I see my cousin's ghost,
Seeking out Romeo that did spit his body
Upon a rapier's point. Stay, Tybalt, stay!
Romeo, I come! this do I drink to thee. 60

She falls on her bed

Scene 4 [*The hall in Capulet's house*]
                    Enter LADY CAPULET *and* NURSE
LADY CAPULET Hold, take these keys and fetch more
          spices, Nurse.
NURSE They call for dates and quinces in the pastry.
                    Enter CAPULET
CAPULET Come, stir, stir, stir! the second cock hath crowed,
      The curfew bell hath rung, 'tis three o'clock. 5
      Look to the baked meats, good Angelica.

At some hours in the night, spirits gather—
Alas, alas. Is it not likely that I,
Waking too early, what with loathsome smells
And shrieks like mandrakes make when torn from earth
That living mortals hearing them, go mad—   50
Oh, if I awake, won't I go mad
Surrounded by all these hideous fears,
And play insanely with my ancestors' bones,
And take the mangled Tybalt from his shroud,
And in this rage, with some great kinsman's bone   55
Used as a club, dash out my despairing brains?
Oh look! I think I see my cousin's ghost
Searching for Romeo who impaled his body
Upon his sword's point! Stop, Tybalt! stop!
Romeo, I come. I drink to you!   60

She falls on her bed

Scene 4 [*The hall in Capulet's house*]

                    Enter LADY CAPULET *and* NURSE

LADY CAPULET Wait, Nurse, take these keys and get more
        spices.

NURSE They're asking for dates and quinces for the pastry.

                    Enter CAPULET

CAPULET Come, hurry up, move, the second rooster has crowed!
        The morning bell has rung; it's three o'clock.   5
        See to the meat pies, good Angelica.

Spare not for cost.

NURSE Go, you cot-quean, go.

Get you to bed. Faith, you'll be sick tomorrow

For this night's watching.   10

CAPULET No, not a whit. What! I have watched ere now

All night for lesser cause, and ne'er been sick.

LADY CAPULET Ay, you have been a mouse-hunt in your time.

But I will watch you from such watching now.

Exit LADY CAPULET *and* NURSE

CAPULET A jealous hood, a jealous hood!   15

Enter some SERVANTS *with spits, logs, and baskets*

Now fellow, what is there?

FIRST SERVANT Things for the cook, sir, I know not what.

Exit FIRST SERVANT

CAPULET Make haste, make haste! Sirrah, fetch drier logs.

Call Peter, he will show thee where they are.

SECOND SERVANT I have a head, sir, that will find out logs   20

And never trouble Peter for the matter.

CAPULET Mass and well said! A merry whoreson, ha!

Thou shalt be loggerhead!

Exit SECOND SERVANT

Good faith! 'Tis day!

The County will be here with music straight,   25

Music within.

For so he said he would. I hear him near.

Nurse! Wife! What ho! What, Nurse, I say!

Enter NURSE

Go waken Juliet, go, and trim her up.

Never mind the expense.

NURSE Off with you, house-husband.

Get to bed. Faith, you'll be sick tomorrow

For staying up all night. 10

CAPULET No, not a bit. Why I have stayed up all night

For lesser reasons and never been sick.

LADY CAPULET Yes, you were a woman-chaser in your day,

But I'll keep you from all that now.

Exit LADY CAPULET and NURSE

CAPULET A jealous woman, a jealous woman! 15

Enter some SERVANTS with spits, logs, and baskets

Now fellow, what have you there?

FIRST SERVANT Some things for the cook. I don't know what all.

Exit FIRST SERVANT

CAPULET Hurry along then, hurry. You there, bring drier logs.

Call Peter, he'll show you where they are.

SECOND SERVANT My head, sir, knows a log when it sees one 20

And needs no help from Peter in this matter.

Exit SECOND SERVANT

CAPULET Fine, well said! You're a clever rascal. Ha, Ha.

We shall call you blockhead.

Heavens, it's day already!

Count Paris will be here with the musicians 25

Music is heard.

As he promised. I can hear them now.

Nurse! Wife! Hello there! Nurse, hello!

Enter NURSE

Go waken Juliet, go and get her dressed.

I'll go and chat with Paris. Hie, make haste,
Make haste! the bridegroom he is come already.   30
Make haste I say.

Exeunt

Scene 5 [*Juliet's bedroom*]

Enter NURSE

NURSE Mistress! What, mistress! Juliet! Fast, I warrant her. She—
Why, lamb. Why, lady, fie! You slugabed!
Why, love, I say! Madam! Sweetheart! Why, bride!
What, not a word? You take your pennyworths now.
Sleep for a week; for the next night, I warrant,   5
The County Paris hath set up his rest
That you shall rest but little! God forgive me!
Marry and amen. How sound is she asleep!
I needs must wake her. Madam, madam, madam!
Ay, let the County take you in your bed,   10
He'll fright you up, i'faith. Will it not be?
She opens the bed curtains
What, dressed, and in your clothes, and down again?
I must needs wake you. Lady! Lady! Lady!
Alas, alas! Help, help! My lady's dead!
O well-a-day that ever I was born.   15
Some aqua vitae! Ho! My lord! My lady!

Enter LADY CAPULET

LADY CAPULET What noise is here?

I'll go and chat with Paris. Quick now, hurry,

Hurry along. The bridegroom's here already. 30

Hurry up, I say.

Exit

Scene 5 [*Juliet's bedroom*]

Enter NURSE

NURSE Mistress! Oh, mistress! Juliet! I'll bet she's still fast asleep.

Now, lamb! now lady, shame, you sleepyhead!

Now love, I say! Madam! Sweetheart! Now, bride!

What, not a word? Well, take your naps now,

Sleep enough for a week, because tonight I'm sure 5

Count Paris has resolved

That you will rest very little! God forgive me.

Why, my goodness, how soundly she sleeps.

I'll have to wake her. Madam, madam, madam!

Oh, my, let Count Paris find you in your bed, 10

And he'll scare you awake, I'll say. Won't he?

She opens the bed curtains

What, you dressed and then fell back to sleep?

I really must wake you. Lady, lady, lady!

Oh no, help, help! My lady's dead!

Oh, it was a sad day when I was born. 15

I need some brandy. My lord, my lady!

Enter LADY CAPULET

LADY CAPULET What's all this noise?

NURSE O lamentable day!

LADY CAPULET What is the matter?

NURSE Look, look! O heavy day! 20

LADY CAPULET O me, O me! My child, my only life.

Revive, look up, or I will die with thee.

Help, help! Call help!

Enter CAPULET

CAPULET For shame, bring Juliet forth; her lord is come.

NURSE She's dead, deceased! She's dead! Alack the day! 25

LADY CAPULET Alack the day! She's dead, she's dead, she's dead!

CAPULET Ha! Let me see her. Out alas! She's cold,

Her blood is settled and her joints are stiff.

Life and these lips have long been separated.

Death lies on her like an untimely frost 30

Upon the sweetest flower of all the field.

NURSE O lamentable day!

LADY CAPULET O woeful time!

CAPULET Death, that hath taken her hence to make me wail,

Ties up my tongue and will not let me speak. 35

Enter FRIAR LAWRENCE, PARIS, *and* MUSICIANS

FRIAR LAWRENCE Come, is the bride ready to go to church?

CAPULET Ready to go, but never to return.

O son, the night before thy wedding day

Hath Death lain with thy wife. There she lies,

Flower as she was, deflowered by him. 40

Death is my son-in-law, Death is my heir.

My daughter he hath wedded. I will die,

NURSE Oh, sorrowful day.

LADY CAPULET What is the matter?

NURSE Look, look! Oh, awful day!   20

LADY CAPULET Oh my! Oh my! My child! My only child!

    Wake up, open your eyes, or I'll die too.

    Help, help! Call for help!

                Enter CAPULET

CAPULET Shame on you. Bring Juliet out. Her groom is here.

NURSE She's dead, deceased! She's dead, terrible day.   25

LADY CAPULET Terrible day. She's dead, she's dead, she's dead!

CAPULET What! Let me see her. Oh no! she's cold.

    Her blood is settled, and her limbs are stiff.

    Life has long since passed from these lips.

    Death lies on her like a too early frost   30

    Upon the sweetest flower in all the field.

NURSE Oh, sorrowful day.

LADY CAPULET Yes, sorrowful day.

CAPULET Death that has taken her to make me wail,

    Has tied up my tongue and will not let me speak.   35

      Enter FRIAR LAWRENCE, PARIS, *and* MUSICIANS

FRIAR LAWRENCE Come, is the bride ready to go to church?

CAPULET Ready to go, but never to return.

    Oh, Count, the night before your wedding day

    Death has slept with your bride. There she lies,

    A flower she was, now deflowered by Death.   40

    Death is my son-in-law; Death is my heir.

    He has wedded my daughter. I will die

And leave him all: life, living, all is Death's.

PARIS Have I thought long to see this morning's face,

And doth it give me such a sight as this?   45

LADY CAPULET Accursed, unhappy, wretched, hateful day!

Most miserable hour that e'er Time saw

In lasting labor of his pilgrimage.

But one, poor one, one poor and loving child,

But one thing to rejoice and solace in,   50

And cruel Death hath snatched it from my sight.

NURSE O woe! O woeful, woeful, woeful day!

Most lamentable day, most woeful day

That ever, ever I did yet behold.

O day, O day, O day, O hateful day!   55

Never was seen so black a day as this.

O woeful day, O woeful day!

PARIS Beguiled, divorced, wronged, spited, slain!

Most detestable Death, by thee beguiled,

By cruel, cruel, thee quite overthrown.   60

O love, O life, Not life, but love in death.

CAPULET Despised, distressed, hated, martyred, killed.

Uncomfortable time, why cam'st thou now

To murder, murder our solemnity?

O child, O child! My soul and not my child,   65

Dead art thou. Alack, my child is dead,

And with my child my joys are buried.

FRIAR LAWRENCE Peace, ho, for shame. Confusion's cure

lives not

In these confusions. Heaven and yourself   70

And leave him everything. Life, property, all is Death's.

PARIS Have I looked forward to this dawn,

    That now gives me a sight like this? 45

LADY CAPULET Cursed, unhappy, wretched, hateful day,

    The most miserable hour Time has ever known

    In the unending labor of his journey.

    Only one, poor one, one poor and loving child,

    Only one thing to rejoice and comfort in, 50

    And cruel Death has snatched it from my sight.

NURSE Oh, grief! Oh, sad, sad, sad day.

    Most sorrowful day. Saddest day

    That ever, ever I did yet behold.

    Oh day, Oh day, Oh day, Oh hateful day. 55

    Never was there so black a day as this.

    Oh sorrowful day. Oh sorrowful day.

PARIS Cheated, separated, wronged, injured, slain.

    Most detestable Death, by you deceived,

    By cruel, cruel Death, completely ruined. 60

    Oh, love, Juliet, you're dead but still my love.

CAPULET Despised, distressed, hated, martyred, killed,

    Painful Time, why did you come now

    To murder, murder our celebration?

    Oh, child, Oh, child! My soul, not only my child, 65

    Is dead now. Alas, my child is dead,

    And with my child, my joys are also buried.

FRIAR LAWRENCE Quiet now. Shame on you. Disaster

      is not cured

    By such carrying on. Heaven and yourself 70

Had part in this fair maid; now heaven hath all,

And all the better is it for the maid.

Your part in her you could not keep from death,

But heaven keeps his part in eternal life.

The most you sought was her promotion,   75

For 'twas your heaven she should be advanced;

And weep ye now, seeing she is advanced

Above the clouds, as high as heaven itself?

O in this love you love your child so ill

That you run mad, seeing that she is well.   80

She's not well married that lives married long,

But she's best married that dies married young.

Dry up your tears, and stick your rosemary

On this fair corse, and, as the custom is,

All in her best array bear her to church.   85

For though fond nature bids us all lament,

Yet nature's tears are reason's merriment.

CAPULET All things that we ordained festival

Turn from their office to black funeral:

Our instruments to melancholy bells,   90

Our wedding cheer to a sad burial feast,

Our solemn hymns to sullen dirges change,

Our bridal flowers serve for a buried corse,

And all things change them to the contrary.

FRIAR LAWRENCE Sir, go you in, and madam, go with him,   95

And go, Sir Paris. Everyone prepare

To follow this fair corse unto her grave.

The heavens do lour upon you for some ill;

Shared this fair maid. Now heaven has all,

And that is all the better for the maid.

Your part of her, you could not keep from death,

But heaven keeps its part in eternal life.

You wanted to see her in a good marriage,   75

Your idea of heaven was such success.

So now why weep that she is even higher,

Above the clouds, as high as heaven itself?

You must not truly love your child

If you go mad, seeing she is well off.   80

She's not well married who lives long married,

But she's best married who dies a young bride.

Dry your tears and put flowering herbs

On this fair corpse and, as the custom is,

In all her finery, bear her to church.   85

It is our human nature that makes us all lament,

But nature's tears are reason's merriment.

CAPULET Everything we prepared to be so festive

Turns from its allotted use to that of a mournful funeral:

Our music into melancholy bells,   90

Our wedding dinner to a sad burial feast.

Our wedding hymns change to mournful songs.

Our bridal flowers become funeral wreaths.

All things change to their opposite.

FRIAR LAWRENCE Sir, you go in. Madam, go with him,   95

And go, Sir Paris. Everyone prepare

To follow this fair corpse to her grave.

Heaven seems to frown upon you for some deed.

Move them no more by crossing their high will.

> *Exit all but the* NURSE *and* MUSICIANS, *casting*
> *rosemary on* JULIET *and shutting the curtains*

FIRST MUSICIAN Faith, we may put up our pipes and be gone   100

NURSE Honest good fellows, ah put up, put up,

> For well you know this is a pitiful case.

FIRST MUSICIAN Ay, by my troth, the case may be amended.

> *Exit* NURSE

> *Enter* PETER

PETER Musicians, O musicians, "Heart's Ease," "Heart's Ease."

> O an you will have me live, play "Heart's Ease."   105

FIRST MUSICIAN Why "Heart's Ease"?

PETER O musicians, because my heart itself plays "My heart is
full." O play me some merry dump to comfort me.

FIRST MUSICIAN Not a dump, we! 'Tis no time to play now.

PETER You will not then?   110

FIRST MUSICIAN No.

PETER I will then give it you soundly.

FIRST MUSICIAN What will you give us?

PETER No money, on my faith, but the gleek! I will give you the
minstrel.   115

FIRST MUSICIAN Then will I give you the serving-creature.

PETER Then will I lay the serving-creature's dagger on your
pate. I will carry no crotchets. I'll *re* you, I'll *fa* you. Do you
note me?

FIRST MUSICIAN An you *re* us and *fa* us, you note us.   120

SECOND MUSICIAN Pray you put up your dagger and put out
your wit.

Don't anger heaven further by protesting, I plead.

Exit all but the NURSE *and* MUSICIANS *casting*
rosemary on JULIET *and shutting the curtains*

FIRST MUSICIAN We might as well pack up and go. 100

NURSE Dear good fellows, yes, pack up, pack up,
You can see this is a sorrowful business.

FIRST MUSICIAN Yes, indeed. May things improve.

Exit NURSE

Enter PETER

PETER Musicians, oh musicians, "Heart's Ease," "Heart's Ease."
If you want me to live, play "Heart's Ease." 105

FIRST MUSICIAN Why "Heart's Ease"?

PETER Oh, musicians, because my heart itself plays "My heart aches,"
so play me a merry tune to cheer me up.

FIRST MUSICIAN We can't play a merry tune. This is no time for that.

PETER You won't play it? 110

FIRST MUSICIAN No.

PETER Then I'll give you something.

FIRST MUSICIAN What will you give us?

PETER No money, for certain, but I'll give you a jest.
I'll call you broken-down fiddlers. 115

FIRST MUSICIAN Then I'll call you a lackey.

PETER Then I will play the lackey's dagger on your head. I'll
put up with no nonsense. I'll *re* you, I'll *fa* you.
Do you take note?

FIRST MUSICIAN You *re* us and *fa* us, and you'd better take note! 120

SECOND MUSICIAN Please, put away your dagger and put out
your wit.

PETER   Then have at you with my wit! I will dry-beat you with
an iron wit, and put up my iron dagger. Answer me like men.
[*Sings.*]   *When griping griefs the heart doth wound,*   125
And doleful dumps the mind oppress,
Then music with her silver sound—
Why "silver sound"? Why "music with her silver sound?"
What say you, Simon Catling?

FIRST MUSICIAN   Marry, sir, because silver hath a sweet sound.   130

PETER   Pretty. What say you, Hugh Rebeck?

SECOND MUSICIAN   I say "silver sound" because musicians
sound for silver.

PETER   Pretty too. What say you, James Soundpost?

THIRD MUSICIAN   Faith, I know not what to say.   135

PETER   O, I cry you mercy, you are the singer. I will say for you.
It is "music with her silver sound" because musicians have no
gold for sounding.
Then music with her silver sound
With speedy help doth lend redress.   140

Exit

FIRST MUSICIAN   What a pestilent knave is this same!

SECOND MUSICIAN   Hang him, Jack. Come, we'll in here, tarry
for the mourners, and stay dinner.

Exeunt

PETER Then I'll beat you with wit. I'll beat you with an
    iron wit and put away my iron dagger. Answer like men:
    [*Sings.*]   *When gripping grief the heart does wound,*   125
        And sad songs leave joy behind,
        Then music with her silver sound—
    Why "silver sound"? Why "music with her silver sound"?
    What do you say, Simon Catgut?
FIRST MUSICIAN Well, sir, because music has a sweet sound.   130
PETER Clever. What do you say, Hugh Rebeck?
SECOND MUSICIAN I say "silver sound" because musicians play
    for money.
PETER Clever, too. What do you say, James Soundingboard?
THIRD MUSICIAN Why, I don't know what to say.   135
PETER I beg your pardon. You must be the singer. I'll tell
    you then. It is "music with her silver sound" because musicians
    get no gold for playing.
        Then music with her silver sound
        With speed will soothe the troubled mind.   140
                        Exit PETER
FIRST MUSICIAN What a pest that rascal is.
SECOND MUSICIAN He can go hang, Jack. Come on, let's go in
    here, wait for the mourners, and stay for dinner.
                        Exit

Act Five

Scene 1 [*A street in Mantua*]

Enter ROMEO

ROMEO If I may trust the flattering truth of sleep
My dreams presage some joyful news at hand.
My bosom's lord sits lightly in his throne,
And all this day an unaccustomed spirit
Lifts me above the ground with cheerful thoughts. 5
I dreamt my lady came and found me dead—
Strange dream that gives a dead man leave to think!
And breathed such life with kisses in my lips
That I revived and was an emperor.
Ah me, how sweet is love itself possessed 10
When but love's shadows are so rich in joy.

Enter BALTHASAR, *Romeo's man, in riding boots*

News from Verona! How now, Balthasar,
Dost thou not bring me letters from the friar?
How doth my lady? Is my father well?
How doth my Juliet? That I ask again, 15
For nothing can be ill if she be well.

BALTHASAR Then she is well and nothing can be ill.
Her body sleeps in Capels' monument,
And her immortal part with angels lives.
I saw her laid low in her kindred's vault 20
And presently took post to tell it you.

Act Five

Scene 1   [*A street in Mantu*a]

Enter ROMEO

ROMEO If I can trust the soothing visions of sleep,

My dreams predict some joyful news at hand.

My heart is light in my chest

And all this day an unusual feeling

Has had me walking on air, thinking cheerful thoughts.   5

I dreamed my lady came and found me dead—

A strange dream that allows a dead man to think—

And she breathed such life with her kisses on my lips

That I revived and was an emperor.

Ah me, how sweet it is to have real love,   10

When even dreams of love are so rich in joy.

Enter BALTHASAR, Romeo's man, in riding boots

News from Verona! How are things, Balthasar?

Do you have some letters from the friar?

How is my lady? Is my father well?

How is my Juliet? I ask that again,   15

For nothing can be wrong if she is well.

BALTHASAR Then she is well, and nothing can be wrong.

Her body sleeps in Capulets' tomb

And her immortal soul lives with the angels.

I saw her laid inside her family's vault   20

And I at once sped here by horse to tell you.

211

O pardon me for bringing these ill news,

Since you did leave it for my office, sir.

ROMEO Is it e'en so? Then I defy you, stars!

Thou knowest my lodging. Get me ink and paper,   25

And hire post-horses. I will hence tonight.

BALTHASAR I do beseech you sir, have patience.

Your looks are pale and wild and do import

Some misadventure.

ROMEO Tush, thou art deceived.   30

Leave me, and do the thing I bid thee do.

Hast thou no letters to me from the friar?

BALTHASAR No, my good lord.

ROMEO No matter. Get thee gone.

And hire those horses. I'll be with thee straight.   35

Exit BALTHASAR

Well, Juliet, I will lie with thee tonight.

Let's see for means. O mischief thou art swift

To enter in the thoughts of desperate men.

I do remember an apothecary—

And hereabouts 'a dwells—which late I noted   40

In tattered weeds, with overwhelming brows,

Culling of simples. Meager were his looks.

Sharp misery had worn him to the bones;

And in his needy shop a tortoise hung,

An alligator stuffed, and other skins   45

Of ill-shaped fishes; and about his shelves

A beggarly account of empty boxes,

Green earthen pots, bladders, and musty seeds,

Oh, forgive me for bringing such bad news,

But it was my duty to do so.

ROMEO Is it really true? Then I defy you, Fate!

You know where I'm living. Get me ink and paper,   25

And hire fast horses. I will leave tonight.

BALTHASAR I do implore you, sir, have patience.

You look pale and wild and seem to be headed

For some sort of trouble.

ROMEO Nonsense, you're wrong.   30

Leave me and do what I asked you to.

Haven't you any letters for me from the friar?

BALTHASAR No, my good lord.

ROMEO No matter. Go on now,

And hire those horses. I'll be right with you.   35

                              Exit BALTHASAR

Well, Juliet, I will lie with you tonight.

But how will I do it? Oh mischief, you're quick

To enter the thoughts of desperate men.

I remember a pharmacist

Who lives around here—I noticed him lately,   40

Dressed in ragged clothes, with bushy eyebrows,

Gathering herbs. He looked thin;

Sharp misery had worn him to the bone.

In his shabby shop, he had a tortoise,

A stuffed alligator, and other skins   45

Of misshapen fishes, and on his shelves

Just a few empty boxes,

Green clay pots, pouches, and musty seeds,

Remnants of packthread, and old cakes of roses

Were thinly scattered to make up a show.   50

Noting this penury, to myself I said,

"An if a man did need a poison now,

Whose sale is present death in Mantua,

Here lives a caitiff wretch would sell it him."

O this same thought did but forerun my need,   55

And this same needy man must sell it me.

As I remember, this should be the house.

Being holiday, the beggar's shop is shut.

What ho! apothecary!

Enter APOTHECARY

APOTHECARY Who calls so loud?   60

ROMEO Come hither, man. I see that thou art poor.

Hold, there is forty ducats. Let me have

A dram of poison, such soon-spreading gear

As will disperse itself through all the veins,

That the life-weary taker may fall dead,   65

And that the trunk may be discharged of breath

As violently as hasty powder fired

Doth hurry from the fatal cannon's womb.

APOTHECARY Such mortal drugs I have, but Mantua's law

Is death to any he that utters them.   70

ROMEO Art thou so bare and full of wretchedness,

And fear'st to die? Famine is in thy cheeks,

Need and oppression starveth in thy eyes,

Contempt and beggary hangs upon thy back.

The world is not thy friend, nor the world's law;   75

Remnants of twine, old cakes of rose petals

Were scattered about to form a display.   50

Noting this poverty, I said to myself,

"If ever a man needed a poison,

Whose sale, if caught, brings death in Mantua,

Here lives a miserable wretch who would sell it to him."

Now this thought anticipated my present need,   55

And this same needy man must sell it to me.

As I remember, this should be the house.

Being a holiday, the beggar's shop is shut.

I'll call him: pharmacist!

          Enter PHARMACIST

PHARMACIST   Who calls so loud?   60

ROMEO   Come here, man. I see you are poor.

    Look, here's forty gold coins. Let me have

    A dose of poison, some quick-acting stuff,

    That will spread itself through the veins,

    So the tired-of-life taker can fall dead,   65

    And so the body can expel its breath

    As quickly as fired gun powder

    Hurries out from the deadly cannon's womb.

PHARMACIST   I have such fatal drugs, but Mantua's law

    Carries a death sentence to anyone who deals in them.   70

ROMEO   Can you be so poor, so wretched, and still be

    Afraid to die? Your cheeks are sunken,

    Hunger and depression show in your eyes.

    Contempt and beggary weighs down your back.

    The world is not your friend, nor the world's laws.   75

The world affords no law to make thee rich;
Then be not poor, but break it, and take this.
APOTHECARY My poverty, but not my will, consents.
ROMEO I pay thy poverty and not thy will.
APOTHECARY Put this in any liquid thing you will   80
    And drink it off, and if you had the strength
    Of twenty men it would dispatch you straight.
ROMEO There is thy gold—worse poison to men's souls,
    Doing more murder in this loathsome world
    Than these poor compounds that thou mayst not sell.   85
    I sell thee poison, thou hast sold me none.
    Farewell, buy food, and get thyself in flesh.
    Come cordial; and not poison, go with me
    To Juliet's grave, for there must I use thee.

                                        Exeunt

Scene 2 [*Friar Lawrence's cell*]
                        Enter FRIAR JOHN
FRIAR JOHN Holy Franciscan Friar, Brother, ho!
                    Enter FRIAR LAWRENCE
FRIAR LAWRENCE This same should be the voice of Friar John.
    Welcome from Mantua. What says Romeo?
    Or, if his mind be writ, give me his letter.
FRIAR JOHN Going to find a barefoot brother out,   5
    One of our order, to associate me,

The world has no law to make you rich,

So don't be poor, break the law, and take this.

PHARMACIST My poverty, against my will, consents.

ROMEO It's your poverty, not your will, I'm paying.

PHARMACIST Put this in any liquid that you choose,   80

Then drink it down, and even if you had the strength

Of twenty men, it would kill you instantly.

ROMEO There's your gold—worse poison to men's souls,

Doing more murder in this loathsome world

Than these pathetic mixtures you're forbidden to sell.   85

I sell you poison, you have sold me none.

Farewell, buy food, and put some flesh on your bones.

This is tonic, not poison. I'll take it

To Juliet's grave, and there I must use it.

Exit

Scene 2 [*Friar Lawrence's cell*]

Enter FRIAR JOHN

FRIAR JOHN Holy Franciscan Friar, Brother, hello.

Enter FRIAR LAWRENCE

FRIAR LAWRENCE That sounds like the voice of Friar John.

Welcome from Mantua. What does Romeo say?

Or, if he has written, give me his letter.

FRIAR JOHN I was looking for another brother monk,   5

One of our order to accompany me,

Here in this city visiting the sick,
And finding him, the searchers of the town,
Suspecting that we both were in a house
Where the infectious pestilence did reign,   10
Sealed up the doors and would not let us forth,
So that my speed to Mantua there was stayed.

FRIAR LAWRENCE   Who bare my letter then to Romeo?

FRIAR JOHN   I could not send it—here it is again—
Nor get a messenger to bring it thee,   15
So fearful were they of infection.

FRIAR LAWRENCE   Unhappy fortune! By my brotherhood,
The letter was not nice but full of charge,
Of dear import, and the neglecting it
May do much danger. Friar John, go hence,   20
Get me an iron crow and bring it straight
Unto my cell.

FRIAR JOHN   Brother, I'll go and bring it thee.

Exit

FRIAR LAWRENCE   Now must I to the monument alone.
Within this three hours will fair Juliet wake   25
She will beshrew me much that Romeo
Hath had no notice of these accidents.
But I will write again to Mantua,
And keep her at my cell till Romeo come.
Poor living corse, closed in a dead man's tomb.   30

Exit

Who was in this city visiting the sick,
And finding him, the health officials,
Suspecting we were both in a house
Where the dread contagious plague dwelled, 10
Boarded up the doors and would not let us out.
So that my rushed trip to Mantua ended right there.
FRIAR LAWRENCE   Then who took my letter to Romeo?
FRIAR JOHN   I couldn't send it. Here it is back.
And I couldn't get any one to bring it to you, 15
Because they were all afraid of infection.
FRIAR LAWRENCE   What misfortune! By my priesthood,
That wasn't a trivial letter, but one full of news
Of great importance, and being undelivered
May cause much damage. Friar John, go out, 20
Get me a crowbar and bring it straight ˙
Back to my cell.
FRIAR JOHN   Brother, I'll go and bring it here.

Exit FRIAR JOHN

FRIAR LAWRENCE   Now, I must go to the tomb all alone.
Within three hours will fair Juliet awake. 25
She'll put heavy blame on me that Romeo
Doesn't know what's been going on.
But I will write again to Mantua,
And keep her at my cell until Romeo comes.
Poor living corpse, closed up in a dead man's tomb. 30

Exit

Scene 3 [*The Capulets' vault*]

Enter PARIS *and his* PAGE, *bearing flowers and a torch*

PARIS Give me thy torch, boy. Hence and stand aloof.

Yet put it out, for I would not be seen.

Under yond yew trees lay thee all along,

Holding thy ear close to the hollow ground;

So shall no foot upon the churchyard tread,   5

Being loose, unfirm with digging up of graves,

But thou shalt hear it. Whistle then to me

As signal that thou hear'st something approach.

Give me those flowers. Do as I bid thee, go.

PAGE I am almost afraid to stand alone   10

Here in the churchyard. Yet I will adventure.

Retires

PARIS *strews the tomb with flowers*

PARIS Sweet flower, with flowers thy bridal bed I strew.

O woe, thy canopy is dust and stones,

Which with sweet water nightly I will dew,

Or wanting that, with tears distilled by moans.   15

The obsequies that I for thee will keep

Nightly shall be to strew thy grave and weep.

PAGE *whistles*

The boy gives warning something doth approach.

What cursed foot wanders this way tonight,

To cross my obsequies and true love's rite?   20

Scene 3 [*The Capulets' vault*]

　　　　Enter PARIS *and his* PAGE, *bearing flowers and a torch*

PARIS Bring me a light, boy, then stand over there.

No, put it out; I don't want to be seen.

Stretch out over there under the yew trees

And put your ear close to the hollow ground

So that if anyone sets foot in the churchyard,　　　　　　　5

Unfirm and loose from digging up of graves,

You'll hear him. Then whistle to me

To signal that you hear someone approach.

Give me those flowers and do as I said. Go on.

PAGE I'm almost afraid to stay alone　　　　　　　　　　10

Here in the graveyard. But I'll be brave.

　　　　　　　　　　　　　　　　PAGE *retires*

PARIS *strews the tomb with flowers*

PARIS Sweet flower, with flowers your bridal bed I strew.

How sad your canopy is dust and stones,

Which I'll mist each night with perfume like dew,

Or if not that, then with misting tears from moans.　　　15

In mourning you, these acts I pledge to keep

To come here nightly with some flowers and weep.

PAGE *whistles*

My page is signaling that someone approaches.

What cursed foot wanders this way tonight

To interrupt my mourning and prayers for my true love?　20

What, with a torch? Muffle me, night, awhile.

PARIS *retires*

Enter ROMEO *and* BALTHASAR *with a torch, a mattock, and a crow of iron*

ROMEO   Give me that mattock and the wrenching-iron.

Hold, take this letter. Early in the morning

See thou deliver it to my lord and father.

Give me the light. Upon thy life I charge thee,   25

Whate'er thou hear'st or seest, stand all aloof,

And do not interrupt me in my course.

Why I descend into this bed of death

Is partly to behold my lady's face,

But chiefly to take thence from her dead finger   30

A precious ring, a ring that I must use

In dear employment. Therefore hence, be gone.

But if thou, jealous, dost return to pry

In what I farther shall intend to do,

By heaven I will tear thee joint by joint,   35

And strew this hungry churchyard with thy limbs.

The time and my intents are savage-wild,

More fierce and more inexorable far

Than empty tigers or the roaring sea.

BALTHASAR   I will be gone, sir, and not trouble ye.   40

ROMEO   So shalt thou show me friendship. Take thou that.

Live and be prosperous, and farewell, good fellow.

BALTHASAR [*Aside*]   For all this same, I'll hide me hereabout.

His looks I fear, and his intents I doubt.

BALTHASAR *retires*

And with a light? Night, hide me for awhile.

PARIS *retires*

Enter ROMEO *and* BALTHASAR *with a light, a pick, and a crowbar*

ROMEO Give me that pick and the crowbar, too.

Here, take this letter and early in the morning

Make sure you deliver it to my lord and father.

Give me the light. Upon your life, I warn you,   25

That whatever you may see or hear, keep away

And do not interrupt me in what I do.

Why I descend into this bed of death

Is partly to behold my lady's face,

But mainly to take from her dead finger   30

A precious ring, a ring that I must use

In a personal matter. Therefore, out, be gone.

But if you, worried, should return to pry

Into what I further intend to do,

By heaven, I will tear you limb from limb   35

And throw your parts about this churchyard, hungry for more bodies.

It's late at night and my intentions are wild,

More fierce and far more determined

Than hungry tigers or the roaring sea.

BALTHASAR I will be gone, sir, and not bother you.   40

ROMEO That will show you are my friend. Take this money,

Live and be prosperous. Farewell, good fellow.

BALTHASAR [*Aside*] All the same, I'll hide nearby.

His looks disturb me, and I fear his intentions.

BALTHASAR *retires*

ROMEO Thou detestable maw, thou womb of death   45

    Gorged with the dearest morsel of the earth,

    Thus I enforce thy rotten jaws to open,

    And in despite I'll cram thee with more food!

ROMEO *opens the tomb*

PARIS [*Aside*] This is that banished haughty Montague

    That murdered my love's cousin—with which grief   50

    It is supposed the fair creature died—

    And here is come to do some villainous shame

    To the dead bodies. I will apprehend him,

    [*Aloud*] Stop thy unhallowed toil, vile Montague.

    Can vengeance be pursued further than death?   55

    Condemned villain, I do apprehend thee.

    Obey and go with me, for thou must die.

ROMEO I must indeed, and therefore came I hither.

    Good gentle youth, tempt not a desperate man.

    Fly hence and leave me. Think upon these gone.   60

    Let them affright thee. I beseech thee, youth.

    Put not another sin upon my head

    By urging me to fury. O be gone!

    By heaven, I love thee better than myself,

    For I come hither armed against myself.   65

    Stay not, be gone, live, and hereafter say,

    A madman's mercy bid thee run away.

PARIS I do defy thy conjuration,

    And apprehend thee for a felon here.

ROMEO Wilt thou provoke me? Then have at thee, boy!   70

They fight

ROMEO You gaping gut, you womb of death,   45

    Gorged with the dearest morsel of this earth.

    Thus do I force your rotten jaws to open,

    And in revenge, I'll cram you with more food.

ROMEO *opens the tomb*

PARIS [*Aside*] This is that arrogant banished Montague

    That murdered my love's cousin, whose death   50

    Caused fair Juliet to die of grief.

    And now he's here to do some wickedness

    To the dead bodies. I will arrest him.

    [*Aloud*] Stop this unholy work, vile Montague.

    Can revenge be pursued past the grave?   55

    Condemned villain, I've caught you.

    Obey and come with me. You must die.

ROMEO I must, indeed, and that's why I came here.

    Good gentle youth, don't provoke a desperate man.

    Go away and leave me alone. Think about those who lie here;   60

    Let them frighten you. I beg you, young man,

    Don't put another sin on my soul

    By prodding me to anger. Oh, please go away!

    By heaven, I love you better than myself,

    For I came here to harm myself.   65

    Don't stay, go away, live, and later on say

    That a madman's mercy let you run away.

PARIS I reject all your earnest appeals

    And arrest you as a felon.

ROMEO Will you provoke me? Then take this, boy!   70

They fight

PAGE O Lord, they fight. I will go call the Watch.

Exit PAGE

PARIS O I am slain! If thou be merciful,
    Open the tomb, lay me with Juliet.

PARIS *dies*

ROMEO In faith I will. Let me peruse this face.
    Mercutio's kinsman, noble County Paris!   75
    What said my man, when my betossed soul
    Did not attend him, as we rode? I think
    He told me Paris should have married Juliet.
    Said he not so? Or did I dream it so?
    Or am I mad, hearing him talk of Juliet,   80
    To think it was so? O give me thy hand,
    One writ with me in sour misfortune's book.
    I'll bury thee in a triumphant grave.
    A grave? O no, a lantern, slaughtered youth.
    For here lies Juliet, and her beauty makes   85
    This vault a feasting presence, full of light.
    Death, lie thou there, by a dead man interred.

[*Lays* PARIS *in the tomb*]

    How oft when men are at the point of death
    Have they been merry! Which their keepers call
    A light'ning before death. O how may I   90
    Call this a light'ning? O my love, my wife,
    Death that hast sucked the honey of thy breath
    Hath no power yet upon thy beauty.
    Thou art not conquered. Beauty's ensign yet
    Is crimson in thy lips and in thy cheeks,   95
    And Death's pale flag is not advanced there.

PAGE Oh Lord! They're fighting! I'll go call the law.

Exit PAGE

PARIS Oh! I am slain! If you have any mercy,

Open up the tomb and place me next to Juliet.

PARIS *dies*

ROMEO I promise, I will. Let me see who you are.

Mercutio's kinsman, the noble Count Paris!   75

What was it my servant said as we rode here

And I was paying no attention? I think

He told me Paris was to marry Juliet.

Did he say that? Or did I just dream it?

Or am I crazy—hearing him talk of Juliet—   80

To think it was so? Oh, give me your hand.

Your name is written with mine in misfortune's book.

I'll bury you in a splendid grave.

A grave? Oh, no a tower dome, slaughtered youth,

For Juliet lies here, and her beauty makes   85

This vault a banquet hall, full of light.

Dead youth, lie there, placed by a dead man.

[*Lays* PARIS *in the tomb*]

How often, when men are at the point of death,

Have they been cheerful. Nurses call that

A lightening before death. How could I call   90

This gloom a lightening? Oh, my love, my wife,

Death may have sucked the honey of your breath

But it hasn't harmed your beauty yet.

You're not conquered by it. Beauty's sign

Is still in your crimson lips and cheeks,   95

And death's pale flag is not yet planted there.

Tybalt, liest thou there in thy bloody sheet?

O, what more favor can I do to thee

Than with that hand that cut thy youth in twain

To sunder his that was thine enemy? 100

Forgive me, cousin. Ah, dear Juliet,

Why art thou yet so fair? Shall I believe

That unsubstantial Death is amorous,

And that the lean abhorred monster keeps

Thee here in dark to be his paramour? 105

For fear of that I still will stay with thee,

And never from this palace of dim night

Depart again. Here, here will I remain

With worms that are thy chambermaids. O here

Will I set up my everlasting rest 110

And shake the yoke of inauspicious stars

From this world-wearied flesh. Eyes, look your last.

Arms, take your last embrace. And lips, O you

The doors of breath, seal with a righteous kiss

A dateless bargain to engrossing Death. 115

[*Takes out the poison*] Come, bitter conduct, come unsavory guide,

Thou desperate pilot now at once run on

The dashing rocks thy seasick weary bark.

Here's to my love! [*Drinks the poison*] O true apothecary!

Thy drugs are quick. Thus with a kiss I die. 120

He falls

       Enter FRIAR LAWRENCE *with lantern, crowbar, and spade*

FRIAR LAWRENCE Saint Francis be my speed. How oft tonight

    Have my old feet stumbled at graves. Who's there?

Tybalt, is that you there in that bloody sheet?

What better favor can I do for you

Than with that hand that cut your youth in half

To cut the youth of him that was your enemy?   100

Forgive me, cousin. Ah, dear Juliet,

Why do you still look so fair? Should I think

That shadowy Death loves you

And that the lean, hated monster keeps

You here in the dark to be his mistress?   105

For fear of that I'll stay here with you,

And never leave this deathbed of dim night,

Never again. Here, here I'll remain with

Worms that are your chambermaids. Oh, here

Will I settle myself for everlasting rest   110

And never more have to suffer what fate sends

To my world-weary flesh. Eyes, look for the last time.

Arms, embrace for the last time, and lips, you

Doorway of my breath, seal with a virtuous kiss

An everlasting bargain with grasping Death.   115

[*Takes out poison*] Come, bitter conductor, unsavory guide,

You desperate pilot, run on the crushing rocks

This weary seasick ship.

Here's to my love! [*Drinks the poison*] Oh, honest pharmacist,

Your drug is quick. I die with a kiss.   120

He falls

    Enter FRIAR LAWRENCE *with light, crowbar, and spade*

FRIAR LAWRENCE Saint Francis speed me on my way. How often tonight

My old feet have stumbled over graves. Who's there?

BALTHASAR Here's one, a friend, and one that knows you well.

FRIAR LAWRENCE Bliss be upon you. Tell me, good my friend,
What torch is yond that vainly lends his light   125
To grubs and eyeless skulls? As I discern,
It burneth in the Capels' monument.

BALTHASAR It doth so, holy sir, and there's my master,
One that you love.

FRIAR LAWRENCE Who is it?   130

BALTHASAR Romeo.

FRIAR LAWRENCE How long hath he been there?

BALTHASAR Full half an hour.

FRIAR LAWRENCE Go with me to the vault.

BALTHASAR I dare not, sir.   135
My master knows not but I am gone hence,
And fearfully did menace me with death
If I did stay to look on his intents.

FRIAR LAWRENCE Stay then, I'll go alone. Fear comes upon me.
O, much I fear some ill unthrifty thing.   140

BALTHASAR As I did sleep under this yew tree here,
I dreamt my master and another fought,
And that my master slew him.

FRIAR LAWRENCE Romeo!

FRIAR LAWRENCE *stoops and looks on the blood and weapons*
Alack, alack, what blood is this which stains   145
The stony entrance of this sepulchre?
What mean these masterless and gory swords
To lie discolored by this place of peace?
Romeo! O, pale! Who else? What, Paris too?

BALTHASAR Here is a friend, and one who knows you well.

FRIAR LAWRENCE Bless you. Tell me, my good friend,

    Whose light is that over there that seems 125

    Wasted on worms and eyeless skulls? It seems to me

    It burns inside the Capulet tomb.

BALTHASAR It does so, holy sir, and that's my master there,

    One whom you love.

FRIAR LAWRENCE Who is it? 130

BALTHASAR Romeo.

FRIAR LAWRENCE How long has he been there?

BALTHASAR At least half an hour.

FRIAR LAWRENCE Come with me to the vault.

BALTHASAR I dare not, sir. 135

    My master thinks that I've gone away,

    And he threatened me with death

    If I stayed to spy on what he would do.

FRIAR LAWRENCE Stay, then, I'll go alone. I'm afraid now,

    Afraid something dreadful has happened. 140

BALTHASAR As I slept under this yew tree here

    I dreamed my master fought with someone,

    And that my master killed him.

FRIAR LAWRENCE Romeo!

FRIAR LAWRENCE *stoops and looks at the blood and weapons*

    Oh no, oh no, Whose blood is it that stains 145

    The stony entrance to this tomb?

    What can this mean, these gory swords lying here

    In this place of peace?

    Romeo! Oh, he's pale. Who else is here? Paris, too?

And steeped in blood? Ah what an unkind hour 150
Is guilty of this lamentable chance?
The lady stirs.

JULIET *rises*

JULIET O comfortable Friar, where is my lord?
I do remember well where I should be,
And there I am. Where is my Romeo? 155

FRIAR LAWRENCE I hear some noise. Lady, come from that nest
Of death, contagion, and unnatural sleep.
A greater power than we can contradict
Hath thwarted our intents. Come, come away.
Thy husband in thy bosom there lies dead, 160
And Paris too. Come, I'll dispose of thee
Among a sisterhood of holy nuns.
Stay not to question, for the Watch is coming.
Come, go, good Juliet. I dare no longer stay.

JULIET Go, get thee hence, for I will not away. 165

Exit FRIAR LAWRENCE

What's here? A cup closed in my true love's hand?
Poison, I see, hath been his timeless end.
O churl, drunk all, and left no friendly drop
To help me after? I will kiss thy lips.
Haply some poison yet doth hang on them. 170
To make me die with a restorative. [*She kisses him*]
Thy lips are warm!

FIRST WATCHMAN [*Outside*] Lead, boy. Which way?

JULIET Yea, noise? Then I'll be brief. O happy dagger.

[*She takes Romeo's dagger, stabs herself, and falls*]
This is thy sheath. There rest, and let me die. 175

And soaked in blood. Oh, what unnatural hour 150

Has caused this sorrowful event?

The lady stirs.

JULIET *rises*

JULIET Oh, comforting Friar, where is my lord?

I remember well where I should be,

And here I am. Where is my Romeo? 155

FRIAR LAWRENCE I hear some noise. Lady, come from that bed

Of death, contagion, and unnatural sleep.

A greater power than we can oppose

Has thwarted our intentions. Come away.

Your husband lies there dead 160

And Paris too. Come, I'll arrange for you

To live in a convent of holy nuns.

Don't wait to ask questions, the Guard is coming.

Come with me, good Juliet. I dare not stay longer.

JULIET You go on, but I must stay here. 165

Exit FRIAR LAWRENCE

What's this? A cup closed in my true love's hand?

Poison, I see, has been his early end.

Oh, stingy. You drank it all and left no friendly drop

To help me follow you. I will kiss your lips.

Perhaps some poison has clung to them 170

To make me die with its helpful medicine. [*Kisses him*]

Your lips are warm.

FIRST WATCHMAN [*Outside*] Lead on, boy. Which way?

JULIET Noise? Then I'll hurry. Oh lucky dagger,

[*She takes Romeo's dagger, stabs herself, and falls*]

I'll be your sheath. Rest here and let me die. 175

Enter PAGE *and* WATCHMEN

PAGE   This is the place. There, where the torch doth burn.

FIRST WATCHMAN   The ground is bloody. Search about
    the churchyard.

    Go, some of you: whoe'er you find, attach.

Exit some WATCHMEN

    Pitiful sight! Here lies the County slain   180

    And Juliet bleeding, warm and newly dead,

    Who here hath lain this two days buried.

    Go tell the Prince. Run to the Capulets.

    Raise up the Montagues. Some others search.

Exit some WATCHMEN

    We see the ground whereon these woes do lie,   185

    But the true ground of all these piteous woes

    We cannot without circumstance descry.

Enter several WATCHMEN with BALTHASAR

SECOND WATCHMAN   Here's Romeo's man. We found him in
    the churchyard.

FIRST WATCHMAN   Hold him in safety till the Prince come hither.   190

Enter another WATCHMAN with FRIAR LAWRENCE

THIRD WATCHMAN   Here is a friar that trembles, sighs, and weeps.

    We took this mattock and this spade from him

    As he was coming from this churchyard's side.

FIRST WATCHMAN   A great suspicion! Stay the friar too.

Enter the PRINCE and ATTENDANTS

PRINCE   What misadventure is so early up,   195

    That calls our person from our morning rest?

Enter PAGE *and* WATCHMEN

PAGE This is the place. There, where that light is burning.

FIRST WATCHMAN The ground is bloody. Search the
    churchyard.
    Go, some of you; arrest anyone you find.

                  Exit some WATCHMEN

    What a pitiful sight! Here lies the dead Count   180
    And Juliet bleeding, warm and just now dead,
    Where she has lain for two days buried.
    Go tell the Prince. Run to the Capulets.
    Awaken the Montagues. Some of you search.

                  Exit some WATCHMEN

    We can see the ground on which these sorrows are revealed, 185
    But the true grounds for all these piteous sorrows
    Are without more details still concealed.

    Enter several WATCHMEN *with* BALTHASAR

SECOND WATCHMAN Here's Romeo's servant. We found him in
    the churchyard.

FIRST WATCHMAN Guard him securely until the Prince gets here.   190

    Enter a WATCHMAN *with* FRIAR LAWRENCE

THIRD WATCHMAN Here is a friar who trembles, sighs, and weeps.
    We took this crowbar and spade from him
    As he was coming from this side of the churchyard.

FIRST WATCHMAN That's highly suspicious. Hold the friar too.

    Enter the PRINCE *and* ATTENDANTS

PRINCE What misfortune is up so early   195
    That calls us from our morning's rest?

Enter CAPULET, LADY CAPULET, *and* SERVANTS

CAPULET What should it be that is so shrieked abroad?

LADY CAPULET O, the people in the street cry "Romeo,"
    Some "Juliet," and some "Paris," and all run
    With open outcry toward our monument.   200

PRINCE What fear is this which startles in your ears?

FIRST WATCHMAN Sovereign, here lies the County Paris slain,
    And Romeo dead, and Juliet, dead before,
    Warm and new killed.

PRINCE Search, seek, and know how this foul murder comes.   205

FIRST WATCHMAN Here is a friar, and slaughtered Romeo's man,
    With instruments upon them fit to open
    These dead men's tombs.

CAPULET O heavens! O wife, look how our daughter bleeds!
    This dagger hath mista'en, for lo, his house   210
    Is empty on the back of Montague,
    And is mis-sheathed in my daughter's bosom.

LADY CAPULET O me! This sight of death is as a bell
    That warns my old age to a sepulchre.

Enter MONTAGUE *and* SERVANTS

PRINCE Come, Montague, for thou art early up   215
    To see thy son and heir now early down.

MONTAGUE Alas, my liege, my wife is dead tonight.
    Grief of my son's exile stopped her breath.
    What further woe conspires against mine age?

PRINCE Look, and thou shalt see.   220

Enter CAPULET, LADY CAPULET, *and* SERVANTS

CAPULET   What is everyone shouting about?

LADY CAPULET   Oh, the people in the street are shouting "Romeo,"

    Some "Juliet," and some "Paris," and they all run

    Shouting toward our family tomb.   200

PRINCE   What news is this that has so alarmed everyone?

FIRST WATCHMAN   Majesty, Count Paris lies here killed,

    And Romeo is dead and Juliet, dead before,

    Is now warm and newly killed.

PRINCE   Search, seek, and learn how this foul murder happened.   205

FIRST WATCHMAN   Here are a friar and murdered Romeo's servant,

    Carrying tools with them to open

    These dead men's tombs.

CAPULET   Oh, heavens, wife, look how our daughter bleeds!

    This dagger has missed its mark. For look, its sheath   210

    Is empty on the back of Montague,

    And wrongly sheathed inside our daughter's breast.

LADY CAPULET   Oh me! This sight of death is like a bell

    That calls me in my old age to the grave.

Enter MONTAGUE *and* SERVANTS

PRINCE   Come, Montague, for you were early raised   215

    To see your son and heir early downed.

MONTAGUE   Alas, my lord, my wife has died tonight.

    Grief over my son's exile has stopped her breath;

    What further disaster threatens my old age?

PRINCE   Look, and you shall see.   220

MONTAGUE O thou untaught! What manners is in this,
    To press before thy father to a grave?
PRINCE Seal up the mouth of outrage for awhile
    Till we can clear these ambiguities
    And know their spring, their head, their true descent,   225
    And then will I be general of your woes
    And lead you, even to death. Meantime forbear,
    And let mischance be slave to patience.
    Bring forth the parties of suspicion.
FRIAR LAWRENCE I am the greatest, able to do least,   230
    Yet most suspected, as the time and place
    Doth make against me, of this direful murder.
    And here I stand, both to impeach and purge
    Myself condemned and myself excused.
PRINCE Then say at once what thou dost know in this.   235
FRIAR LAWRENCE I will be brief, for my short date of breath
    Is not so long as is a tedious tale.
    Romeo, there dead, was husband to that Juliet,
    And she, there dead, that Romeo's faithful wife.
    I married them, and their stolen marriage-day   240
    Was Tybalt's doomsday, whose untimely death
    Banished the new-made bridegroom from this city;
    For whom, and not for Tybalt, Juliet pined.
    You, to remove that siege of grief from her,
    Betrothed and would have married her perforce   245
    To County Paris. Then comes she to me
    And with wild looks bid me devise some means
    To rid her from this second marriage,

MONTAGUE Oh, how rude! What manners are these, son,
　　To push ahead of your father to the grave?
PRINCE Seal up the mouth of outcry for a time,
　　Till we can clear up the mysteries
　　And know their source, their cause, their origin,　　　225
　　And then I will be the leader of your mourning
　　As long as you live. Meanwhile, be calm
　　And let your distress be ruled by patience.
　　Now, bring the suspects before me.
FRIAR LAWRENCE I am the oldest, yet can do the least,　　　230
　　The most suspected because of time and place.
　　Both go against me in this dreadful murder.
　　And here I stand, ready to accuse, then clear,
　　My name. Condemned and excused by myself.
PRINCE Then say what you know about this immediately.　　　235
FRIAR LAWRENCE I'll be brief, for what remains of my life
　　Is not so long as a tedious tale.
　　Romeo, lying there dead, was married to Juliet
　　And she, dead too, was Romeo's faithful wife.
　　I married them, and their secret wedding day　　　240
　　Was Tybalt's last day, whose early death
　　Banished the new bridegroom from this city.
　　Juliet pined for him, not for Tybalt.
　　You, to stop her grieving so much,
　　Betrothed and would have married her by force　　　245
　　To the Count Paris. Then she came to see me
　　And with wild looks begged me to think of some plan
　　To save her from this second marriage,

Or in my cell there would she kill herself.
Then gave I her—so tutored by my art—   250
A sleeping potion, which so took effect
As I intended, for it wrought on her
The form of death. Meantime I writ to Romeo
That he should hither come as this dire night
To help to take her from her borrowed grave,   255
Being the time the potion's force should cease.
But he which bore my letter, Friar John,
Was stayed by accident, and yesternight
Returned my letter back. Then all alone
At the prefixed hour of her waking   260
Came I to take her from her kindred's vault,
Meaning to keep her closely at my cell
Till I conveniently could send to Romeo.
But when I came, some minutes ere the time
Of her awakening, here untimely lay   265
The noble Paris and true Romeo dead.
She wakes, and I entreated her come forth
And bear this work of heaven with patience;
But then a noise did scare me from the tomb,
And she, too desperate, would not go with me,   270
But, as it seems, did violence on herself.
All this I know; and to the marriage
Her Nurse is privy; and if aught in this
Miscarried by my fault, let my old life
Be sacrificed, some hour before his time   275

Or she would kill herself there in my cell.

Then I gave her—I learned it in my studies— 250

A sleeping potion; and it worked

As I intended, for it brought on her

The look of death. Meanwhile, I wrote to Romeo

That he should come here this same dreadful night

To help to take her from her borrowed grave, 255

Because by then the potion should have worn away.

But the carrier of my letter, Friar John,

Was kept here by accident, and last night he

Gave me back my letter. So, all alone,

At the hour fixed for her awakening, 260

I came here to take her from her family's tomb,

Meaning to keep her hidden in my cell

Till I found means to send for Romeo.

But when I came here, a few minutes before

Her awakening, there I found 265

The noble Paris and true Romeo, dead before their time.

She awoke, and I begged her to come with me

And bear this work of heaven with acceptance;

But then a noise startled me, and I left the tomb,

And she, so deep in despair, would not go with me, 270

But, as it seems, took her own life.

That is all I know. As for the marriage,

Her Nurse knows all about it too. If anything

Went wrong because of me, let my old life

Be taken before it is time, sacrificed to satisfy 275

Unto the rigor of severest law.

PRINCE   We still have known thee for a holy man.

Where's Romeo's man? What can he say to this?

BALTHASAR   I brought my master news of Juliet's death,

And then in post he came from Mantua   280

To this same place, to this same monument.

This letter he early bid me give his father

And threatened me with death, going in the vault,

If I departed not, and left him there.

PRINCE   Give me the letter, I will look on it.   285

Where is the County's Page, that raised the Watch?

Sirrah, what made your master in this place?

PAGE   He came with flowers to strew his lady's grave,

And bid me stand aloof, and so I did.

Anon comes one with light to ope the tomb,   290

And by and by my master drew on him,

And then I ran away to call the Watch.

PRINCE   This letter doth make good the Friar's words,

Their course of love, the tidings of her death.

And here he writes that he did buy a poison   295

Of a poor apothecary, and therewithal

Came to this vault to die and lie with Juliet.

Where be these enemies? Capulet, Montague,

See what a scourge is laid upon your hate,

That heaven finds means to kill your joys with love.   300

And I, for winking at your discords too

Have lost a brace of kinsmen. All are punished.

The harsh demands of the strictest law.

PRINCE We've always known you to be a pious man.

Where's Romeo's servant? What does he add to this?

BALTHASAR I brought my master news of Juliet's death,

And then he came in haste from Mantua   280

To this very place and this very tomb.

He first gave me this letter for his father,

Then entering the vault, he threatened me with death

If I did not go away and leave him there.

PRINCE Give me the letter. I will look at it.   285

Where is the Count's Page who called the Watchmen?

Tell me, what made your master come to this place?

PAGE He came to lay flowers on his lady's grave

And told me to wait at a distance, and so I did.

Soon someone came, with a light, to open the tomb   290

And by and by my master drew his sword on him,

And then I ran away to call the Watchmen.

PRINCE This letter proves what the Friar said,

Their courtship, the news of her death,

And here he writes that he bought some poison   295

From a poor pharmacist and with that

Came here to this vault to die and lie with Juliet.

Where are those enemies? Capulet, Montague,

See how your hatred has been punished?

Heaven found a way to kill your children through love.   300

And I, for allowing your feud to continue,

Have lost two dear kinsmen. We're all punished.

CAPULET O brother Montague, give me thy hand.
 This is my daughter's jointure, for no more
 Can I demand.   305
MONTAGUE But I can give thee more.
 For I will raise her statue in pure gold,
 That whiles Verona by that name is known,
 There shall no figure at such rate be set
 As that of true and faithful Juliet.   310
CAPULET As rich shall Romeo's by his lady's lie,
 Poor sacrifices of our enmity.
PRINCE A glooming peace this morning with it brings.
 The sun for sorrow will not show his head.
 Go hence to have more talk of these sad things. 315
 Some shall be pardoned, and some punished,
 For never was a story of more woe
 Than this of Juliet and her Romeo.
           Exeunt

CAPULET Oh, brother Montague, give me your hand.

    This is my daughter's wedding gift, for no more

    Can I demand. 305

MONTAGUE But I will give you more,

    For I'll make a statue of her in pure gold,

    And as long as Verona lasts,

    There shall be no statue valued as highly

    As that of true and faithful Juliet. 310

CAPULET I'll place as rich a statue of Romeo by her side,

    Poor victims of our enmity.

PRINCE A gloomy peace this morning brings.

    The sun in sorrow will not show its face.

    Go home to talk more of these sad things. 315

    We'll pardon some, others punish, case by case.

    For never was there a story of more woe

    Than this of Juliet and her Romeo.

Exit

Glossary

The following terms are taken from the translation of *The Tragedy of Romeo and Juliet*. The scene and line numbers are given in parentheses after the terms, which are listed in the order they first occur.

Act One

Verona (Prologue, line 2): a town in northeastern Italy

star-crossed (Prologue, line 6): born under the unfavorable influence of the stars and destined for unhappiness

Cupid (scene 1, line 207): god of love. He is often pictured as a child, blindfolded, carrying a bow and arrows

Diana (scene 1, line 207): the moon goddess, who chose to remain a virgin

plantain leaf (scene 2, line 52): broad leaf used to staunch the flow of blood

Lammastide (scene 3, line 17): a religious festival, beginning August 1, giving thanks for the harvest by blessing the loaves of bread made from the new crop

Mantua (scene 3, line 31): a town in northern Italy, about 25 miles from Verona

Queen Mab (scene 4, line 57): this mythological creature has no known earlier reference, so she is probably Shakespeare's invention

Pentecost (scene 5, line 36): a religious feast occurring fifty days after Easter, celebrating the descent of the Holy Spirit upon the apostles of Christ

palmers (scene 5, line 104): religious pilgrims who carried palm branches to show they had visited the Holy Land

Act Two

Venus (scene 1, line 13): mythological goddess of love and beauty

Echo (scene 2, line 170): the mythological nymph whose unrequited love for Narcissus caused her to waste away until nothing was left but her voice. She lived in caves and could only repeat what others said

Benedicite (scene 3, line 33): Latin for "God bless you"

Prince of Cats   (scene 4, line 18): a play on Tybalt's name, which is close to that of Sir Tybert, the Prince of Cats in the medieval fable *Reynard the Fox*

Petrarch   (scene 4, line 36): fourteenth century Italian poet who wrote love sonnets to an idealized woman, Laura

Dido...Cleopatra...Helen...Hero...Thisbe   (scene 4, lines 37-39): romantic heroines of legend

pinked shoe   (scene 4, line 55): a shoe with small decorative holes

Talley ho!   (scene 4, line 115): the call of a hunter at the sight of a fox

Lent   (scene 4, line 117): a season of fasting and penitence, ending the day before Easter

Act Three

Phaeton   (scene 2, line 3): the son of Phoebus Apollo who was allowed to drive his father's chariot for one day, lost control, and was destroyed by a thunderbolt from Jupiter

cockatrice   (scene 2, line 49): a legendary serpent with the head, wings, and feet of a cock, able to kill with its look

Act Four

mandrakes   (scene 3, line 49): plants whose forked roots make them resemble human figures. They were thought to shriek when pulled from the earth, and anyone hearing the sound supposedly went mad

"Heart's Ease"   (scene 5, line 104): a popular song during Shakespeare's time

re, fa   (scene 5, line 118): the second and fourth notes of the musical scale

rebeck   (scene 5, line 131): a stringed instrument, ancestor of the violin